M000106605

Dear Ms. Demeanor...

Dear Ms. Demeanor...

The Young Person's Etiquette Guide to Handling Any Social Situation with Confidence and Grace

MARY MITCHELL

CB
CONTEMPORARY BOOKS
CHICAGO

Library of Congress Cataloging-in-Publication Data

Mitchell, Mary, 1949–
Dear Ms. Demeanor : the young person's etiquette guide to handling any social situation with confidence and grace / Mary Mitchell.
p. cm.
Includes index
ISBN 0-8092-3630-3
1. Etiquette for children and teenagers. I. Title. II. Title: Dear Miss Demeanor.
BJ1857.C5M54 1994
395'.123—dc20 94-20545
CIP

Published by Contemporary Books, Inc.
Two Prudential Plaza, Chicago, Illinois 60601-6790
Manufactured in the United States of America
International Standard Book Number: 0-8092-3630-3
10 9 8 7 6 5 4 3 2 1

With joy and love, I dedicate this book to
my two best friends . . .
Daniel Fleischmann, my husband and muse
Lillian Mitchell, my sister and sounding board

Contents

Foreword

By now it's no secret that parenting a child to adulthood is one of the most important tasks parents face and one for which there is little or no advance preparation.

Today's parents have the formidable challenge of remaining caring parents and loving spouses while juggling increasing responsibilities at work, the necessities of maintaining a home, and the time needed to be involved in community affairs. Parents tell me they just don't have the energy to police their children in even the basics such as table manners or saying "excuse me" after bumping into someone.

At last, there is help. Mary Mitchell has a storehouse of information for parents, grandparents, and children. Her commonsense answers to the most sensitive questions are geared to the lifestyle of the nineties, but I predict they will be applicable in the twenty-first century, too.

This book should be required reading for all parents who work daily in situations where the basics of etiquette are vital to success but are all too often ignored at home. "Ms. Demeanor" offers advice and direction for handling virtually any situation.

Dorothea Johnson
Director,
The Protocol School of Washington

Preface

ABOUT THIS BOOK

I do not pretend to offer a complete book of etiquette here. That is for the talent of Letitia Baldrige, whose books I probably have committed to memory by now. What you are about to read are the "big questions" concerning the world of etiquette, as viewed through the eyes of children. These are the things children want to know, based on a large nationwide sample.

I do, however, take the study and practice of etiquette very much to heart. The answers put forth here are based on sound principles indeed. They are taken from what I have learned from my years as a professional etiquette instructor, from Ms. Baldrige and from Dorothea Johnson, director of the Protocol School of Washington, D.C., a superb teacher. And it began with an upbringing in a household where both parents were vigilant about such matters.

The interpretation I bring to those principles has, if you will, a spiritual basis: I believe all of us are children of our Creator and therefore worthy of dignity and respect, the two foundation stones of etiquette. I believe (and do my best to live up to that belief) that our Divine Parent gave us a legacy that supersedes the vicissitudes of everyday life, a larger plan to carry us through. I attempt to make this basis evident in my writing and teaching.

This book actually began in 1990, when a stranger named Susan Hedden called to ask if I would be willing to teach a class about manners at the Gesu School, Philadelphia. The school is in the heart of the highest-crime area in the city. The daily lives of the children there include fending off (maybe) drug deals and domestic violence.

I was terrified and intimidated by the prospect of entering a world so diametrically opposed to the one in which I was reared and continue to live, but I said yes. In my private thoughts I knew I would become the student, not the teacher. As it turned out, the call was a prayer answered.

I had been training corporate executives in business etiquette and protocol for some time and had been fortunate enough to receive a good deal of publicity for it. However, the bottom line of each newspaper article suggested that the value of my services was the obvious financial payoff gained from not offending a client or a boss during a business dinner. This type of public attention ignored what I consider the two most valuable benefits of manners and etiquette: self-confidence for those who know the rules; kindness and respect for those on the receiving end. I believe our relationships are our most valuable assets.

This narrow view of my etiquette teaching often made me wonder if I was on the right path. I worried about just what my work was communicating to the world when it was portrayed in such a slam-dunk manner by the media. I prayed for some sign that would tell me whether my view of my own work was worth pursuing, whether it actually helped people feel better about themselves and thus become more effective in their own lives.

I was determined that, however God answered, I would follow, either by continuing to teach etiquette or by letting it go to retreat to a former career in marketing.

In the spring of 1991 I stood in front of a class of children for the first time. I remember feeling ready to break out in hives from anxiety. I remember wondering whether a blond, WASP-looking, East Coast, outwardly elitist etiquette teacher could possibly have anything of interest or meaning to share with them.

I shouldn't have worried. Those children became human sponges, soaking up everything and anything I could teach that might help them improve their lives in the inner city. Never before, or since, have I played to a more respectful, willing, and receptive audience. Never has my knowledge been more appreciated and valued. They captured my heart. What originally was supposed to have been a three-week program continues to this day.

It was during that first program that *Philadelphia Inquirer* feature writer John Corr coaxed me into inviting him to the Gesu School classes. He later told the story in a magazine article headlined "Ms. Demeanor," playing off my pen name on a bylined column I wrote for an area business publication. The magazine article came to the attention of my friend Bob Greenberg, associate managing editor for the *Inquirer*. Bob suggested I write a "Ms. Demeanor" column for kids and submit it. When another *Inquirer* associate managing editor, Ron Patel, gave it the green light, "Ms. Demeanor," as most people now know the column, first saw print.

I have been honored by the confidence and trust that young people place in me. They share their anxieties and insecurities. The more they share, the more I hear them resonate with adult concerns. For example, it is common for a child in my class to confide how worrisome it is to go to a birthday party not knowing who will be there, what to talk about, and with whom. An adult will call my office and ask if my company offers seminars on how to work a room. Same thing, different language.

It then occurred to me that if I could relate the concerns of children about making their relationships work to adult concerns about the same thing, I could build a bridge that anyone could cross. Hence, this book.

Of course, the true motivation behind why I write and speak on the topics of manners and etiquette is that I teach what I want to learn.

Mary Mitchell
Philadelphia
1994

Acknowledgments

SAYING THANK YOU, PROPERLY

No one writes a book alone. I am no exception.

As I wrote this book for parents, I became acutely aware of how grateful I am to my own parents and the rest of the family who, in so many ways, showed me the value, wisdom, and beauty of good manners.

With so few children to learn from in my own family, I am especially grateful to George W. Bur, S.J.; Ed Becket, S.J.; and Linda Filipponi, I.H.M.; for welcoming me into the Gesu School, Philadelphia, and letting me be a small part of their remarkable work. Of course, special thanks to Susan Hedden for discovering me on the school's behalf.

The support of my *Philadelphia Inquirer* family has been inestimable in this process. It was the *Inquirer* that first brought "Ms. Demeanor" to print and provided the forum for letters from children that comprise the bulk of this book. How can I ever thank enough Bob Greenberg and Ron Patel, associate managing editors, for having the idea for the column in the first place and giving it the green light, respectively? My immediate editor, Bob Samsot, is a real gentleman. His judicious editing improved my work and taught me the tremendous gift good editing can be. Further, his perspective as a parent and his droll chiding made me look forward to our talks. That must be what it feels like to have a brother. Finally at the *Inquirer*, I thank Maureen Carman for so patiently inputting all my materials into the newspaper's computer.

Jonathan Kremer gets the credit for inspiring my nom de plume, Ms. Demeanor. I counted on Joan Carson's good-humored perception, patient research, and commentary to keep me focused and to prevent me from wallowing in my insecurities. I have been privileged to have access to Dr. James B. Hoyme, medical director at the Institute of Pennsylvania Hospital. Bob Katzenstein, Betsy Salunek, and Donna Schanel also shared their professional expertise whenever I asked. The entries on Judaism, grief, and disabilities would be hollow without their help. Dan Fleischmann, a distinguished restaurateur, provided invaluable input for all sections dealing with dining.

I have relied heavily on the work and wisdom of the inimitable Letitia Baldrige and Dorothea Johnson, director of the Protocol School of Washington, D.C., for a solid foundation in etiquette and how to teach it. And clearly, I have been influenced mightily by the work of Eleanor Roosevelt. Amid these giants who have come before, I am humbled and proud to be the new kid on the block.

Nancy Love, my agent, has coached me well through the sometimes painful process of my first book. Without my journalist friend Rose De Wolf, we never would have met.

The Reverend John Salunek, John Harricharan, and Jane Dalton have stayed my spiritual course throughout everything I've written and helped me recognize my own higher purpose, and that of everyone I deal with.

Finally I am pleased to thank Dan Eisenhuth, the former editor of *Focus*, Philadelphia's business newsmagazine, for persuading me to tackle this project. Without his contribution of time, editing, and organizational skills there never would have been a book. He also contributed the insights of his two sons, Kurt and Jeffrey Eisenhuth, whom I thank for being my young advisers.

Above all, I extend heartfelt thanks to every young person and adult who wrote to share concerns, criticisms, and comments. I am honored to serve you.

Dear Ms. Demeanor...

1
Manners and Etiquette Begin at Home

"Brothers and sisters are friends given by nature."
French proverb

For parents . . .

When you begin to teach manners and etiquette to children, they will question the rules endlessly and mercilessly. They will want to know what, when, and, above all, why. At first their questions may sound silly or simplistic. They will ask for basics and absolutes. And they will test your patience. But be warned: children ask questions about things adults take for granted, about things so ingrained in our daily lives that we rarely question the rationale behind them ourselves.

The need for a mutually agreed-on set of rules to govern interpersonal conduct (etiquette, for short) is part of the adult life experience. We do not, for example, need to remind ourselves in detail of all the reasons we should not push our way to the front of the checkout line at the supermarket or interrupt the boss in the middle of a speech to employees. Some of us know more, some less, but all functioning adults have picked up parts of this unwritten code along the road of life.

Because adults have learned to handle most social situations on autopilot, we often are not prepared when children want to know exactly *why* we should or should not do certain things. Composing good answers to these basic questions takes careful self-exploration and considerable thought. Your ability to answer your child's questions clearly and with conviction will prove your own commitment to *why* that child should learn proper etiquette.

This chapter (and the rest of this book) is written to give you the words, facts, and reasoning you'll need to be convincing. Having the language to explain why will improve your patience, too. Read, learn, and be able to provide an answer better than the all-too-common but hollow "Because I said so, that's why."

You should know, for example, that etiquette of some sort probably began some eleven thousand years ago, when early humans, switching to farming from hunting and gathering, first sat down to a communal meal. You should know that there is an ancient tradition behind why we break bread before buttering it. You should know that a handshake is more than a greeting. You should know there is a comparatively modern story explaining how and why we use a fork.

Etiquette training begins at home. All parents impart a code of conduct to their children as they interact around the family dining table, at play with brothers and sisters, on the telephone, with relatives and adult visitors, and—as the first and most basic human interaction—with mother and father.

All rules of etiquette are based on respect for fellow human beings. When that respect exists, it follows naturally that people will want to create comfort and ease with others, whether friends or strangers. The rules of etiquette are that simple, but the reasons why may not be as easy to explain.

So let us begin with the really basic stuff, the questions most often asked by boys and girls in the process of learning etiquette, to which even experienced adults may not know the answers.

Remember to say "please," "thank you," "you're welcome," and "excuse me."

Q. ***What are the three most important things to remember about manners?***

A. 1. Be kind. Don't hurt people's feelings.
2. Say, "please," "thank you," "you're welcome," and "excuse me."
3. Look people in the eye when you talk with them.

All of these show respect for others, the main point of manners.

Q. ***Where do manners come from?***

A. More than eleven thousand years ago, people were concerned mainly with hunting and gathering food and finding shelter. There wasn't time in those days to worry about manners. You may be able to imagine what a brutal era that was. Then—about eleven thousand years ago—humans evolved from hunter-gatherers to farmers. Because they no longer had to roam the forests to find and kill game and gather nuts and berries, there was more leisure time. There also was more food from the fields. That food was served at a table where everyone met to eat. When families came together to prepare and consume meals, they created rules of behavior. Those rules became customs and were passed down from generation to generation. The earliest written advice on manners and etiquette ever discovered comes from ancient Egypt. It was written about four thousand years ago by someone named Ptahhotep, an adviser to the Egyptian pharaoh (king) Isesi. The manuscript advises young Egyptians on conversation and table manners! This information comes from a wonderful book titled *Panati's Extraordinary Origins of Everyday Things*, published by Harper & Row in 1987.

Q. ***What's the difference between manners and etiquette?***

A. Etiquette is a set of rules we live by. These rules differ from place to place. One set of rules is really no better than another set. For example, in the United States we shake hands when we meet someone. In Japan, people bow when they meet.

Manners are the way we put those rules into effect. Good manners are based on respect and genuine kindness for other people. The reason to learn etiquette is that knowing how we are expected to behave wherever we are puts us more at ease and enables us to put those around us at ease. Embarrassing someone is bad manners. Always remember that a person's feelings are more important than the rules.

Never miss an opportunity to praise friends and family members.

Q. ***What is the rudest thing you can do?***

A. The rudest thing you can do is hurt someone's feelings. All of us have hot buttons that really hurt when someone else pushes them. All of us feel inadequate about something. We wish we were taller, shorter, thinner, heavier, richer, smarter. Usually the things we don't like about ourselves are things we really cannot change for the most part, so it is doubly painful when someone makes fun of us because of them. Sometimes people cover up their feelings by pretending to poke fun at themselves. That's OK for them, but if you poke fun at them you might hurt them. All of us, children and adults, need to remember to treat people the way we want to be treated. It is much more important than remembering to use the right fork or spoon.

Q. ***Why do I have to shake hands?***

A. The custom of shaking hands goes back centuries to a time when knights bared their hands in greeting to prove they carried no weapons and their intentions were peaceful. Over time the tradition has symbolized the same thing—friendship and goodwill. Shaking hands has become the traditional greeting in the United States. In the American business culture the handshake is the only acceptable form of physical contact, and it is considered very bad manners to refuse an extended hand. In this country we also look a person in the eye when we shake hands and give a good, firm grip. Avoiding someone's gaze or giving a limp handshake is considered a sign of an untrustworthy person.

This is not so in other countries, however. For example, in the Middle East people shake hands very gently because to do otherwise suggests aggression. Direct eye contact is considered disrespectful. Shaking hands is universally accepted in North America and most of Europe. However, there are several variations on what is considered proper in each country. When you're traveling from country to country, it is a good idea to do some homework. One excellent source of this information (that also is lots of fun to read) is a book titled *Gestures* by Roger Axtell and published by John Wiley & Sons, Inc.

Q. ***If I don't really like someone, do I have to shake hands anyway?***

A. Refusing to shake hands is very rude and hurtful. It means you refuse to acknowledge someone, and it has nothing to do with whether you like, approve of, or support that person. Broaden your thinking and consider how professional athletes are willing to shake hands after a game. I'm sure you've also seen tennis matches or races on television where each player has a career and a fortune at stake. Do you think the loser is eager to shake the winner's hand? I doubt it, but the gesture of shaking the victor's hand communicates acknowledgment and respect for the other player's skills.

I'm not telling you to rush to people you don't like and create situations to shake hands just so you can suffer. I am telling you to recognize others as human beings. On that basis, shake a hand when it is extended. It has nothing to do with liking a person.

Q. ***Why is it polite to open doors and pull out chairs for people?***

A. Opening doors and pulling out seats are considered marks of good manners in the United States and much of the rest of the Western world. Good manners will help you gain good friends and enjoy good times with them and other people in your life. The rules of behavior called *etiquette* that dictate what is and is not good manners are different from country to country and society to society, as we just discussed, and they are changing all the time.

The custom of opening doors and pulling out chairs came

to this country from a tradition called *chivalry* that began in the days of knights in armor in Europe. In those old times men showed respect for women by protecting them, holding doors open for them, walking between women and traffic (usually horses in those days) on a street to shield them, and pulling out their chairs from under tables so they could sit down gracefully.

These kindnesses remained pretty much unchallenged and unchanged through the ages until about twenty years ago, when women began to play a larger role in American business life. Feminists rejected such gestures from men as attempts to keep women from gaining equal treatment and, thus, equal power. Many women said they were as capable of looking after themselves as men were.

In today's grown-up world the rule is: whoever needs help should get it, whether it is a man or a woman giving it. Whoever sees the need should provide the help. Think how you feel when someone anticipates your needs and helps you. Pretty good, I bet. It is a way to demonstrate to people in your world that you value and respect them, even if you don't know them.

Opening doors and pulling out chairs are still seen as signs of respect in the United States. The same goes for giving up your own seat for someone older or less robust than you. But there are other things that you might describe as common sense that also are the mark of good manners—something as simple as making sure someone has enough room to pass you in a crowded hallway or when moving to the rear of a bus. Taking the time to use common sense wins half the battle when you're learning good manners and etiquette.

Q. ***Is it rude to return a gift?***

A. Yes and no. If someone gives you a one-of-a-kind gift or something he or she considers very special (especially if the giver made it for you), you must keep it. However, if you received duplicate gifts—two of the same CDs or videos, for example—it is perfectly all right to exchange one, since nobody needs more than one. Sometimes we receive books that we already have read, and they also are all right to return or exchange. Naturally it makes sense to return clothes that don't fit. If the exact color or style is not available, go ahead and choose something else.

If the person who gave you the gift asks about it, tell the truth. Otherwise, don't bring it up. Never ask or expect the person who gave you the gift to exchange it for you.

Above all, be complimentary and enthusiastic about all gifts you receive, even when they are not to your taste. You can do this without telling a lie. Just say something like "What a thoughtful thing for you to do. Thank you so much for picking this out."

Gifts show high regard for you because they represent time and energy spent on your behalf. The most precious gift we can give is our attention. To hurt a friend's feelings after you've been given a gift is a very serious blow.

Respect is earned.
It cannot be purchased.

Q. ***Why do I have to be nice to my parents' friends?***

A. Technically speaking, you don't have to be nice to anyone. You can choose whether you treat people with consideration and respect or with contempt. As a human being, you have free will. I am sure you know many examples of people who do not choose to treat other people respectfully. At one extreme they are called murderers or muggers or criminals. At the other extreme they are just those negative, unpleasant people you don't like to be around. I can give you some direction on how to get along with people better and make your life more harmonious, but I would never tell you that you have to "be nice" or anything else. That would be an insult to your intelligence and free will.

In answer to the question, your mother and father deserve respect simply because they are human beings and, more so, because they are your parents. It follows logically that you would give their friends the same respect and courtesy. This does not mean that you have to like your parents' friends or attempt to make those people your own friends. You just have to make every effort to be considerate, not rude. Say hello and shake hands. Offer refreshments when it makes sense. Acknowledge their presence when you're in the same room together. Think about how you would feel if you were in their place. What kind of treatment would you expect? There is no need for icy stares, rolling your eyes, making faces, or throwing tantrums if you find yourself in the company of people you do not like. Just look for ways to politely avoid the situation.

Another consideration: have you told your parents how you feel about their friends? It is not up to you to choose your parents' friends, but it is fair to tell them honestly how you feel. Do it without anger. Don't make accusations. Be matter-of-fact. Above all, do not attack your parents.

Q. ***Why do I have to wash my hands?***

A. There are a number of reasons. One is that being well-groomed shows that you respect yourself. Another is that by staying clean in general and keeping your hands clean in particular you stop spreading germs that cause colds and other diseases. We can learn a good lesson about the value of cleanliness from cats. Cats instinctively know this grooming rule, especially the big tigers that live in tropical India. They constantly groom themselves because a simple cut on the paw could mean serious infection and possibly death if it is not kept clean. So wash your hands often. Always wash after going to the bathroom and before meals. Dirty hands and fingernails are a really big turnoff to anyone who sees them.

Good grooming becomes more important as the weather gets warmer.

Q. ***Do I have to take a shower every day?***

A. You bet. Here's a good guide for how to start your day, every day:

First, take a shower. Wash your face, ears, and neck. Make sure your fingernails and teeth are clean. Put on clean underwear and fresh clothes (and if you are old enough to read this answer, you're also old enough to learn to do laundry). Make your bed, straighten your room, and leave it neat and clean. Clean up after yourself after you've used the bathroom. Say "good morning" to everyone in your family. If you are responsible for helping others in your family in the morning (perhaps sisters or brothers), start their day off right, too. Feed your pet. Walk it. Give it a hug. Doing all this takes a few extra minutes in the morning, but it is a truly worthwhile way to start your day. Why? Because you're beginning each day by treating yourself and everyone else in your world with respect and kindness.

Q. ***Why do I have to say "excuse me" when parents are talking and I want to say something?***

A. Would you rather just burst in so you can be heard at all costs, interrupting your parents' conversation and thought? Maybe you would, but what would that accomplish? For one thing, instead of hearing what you want to say, your parents will be too irritated by your rudeness to pay attention to you. By butting in, you've defeated yourself before you even got to talk. Not smart, not polite, and not kind.

Q. ***Why isn't it polite to talk back to my parents?***

A. It isn't polite to snap back at anybody, especially your parents, teachers, and other persons in positions of authority. Anything you say in anger or irritation has a lot less force than what you say calmly and thoughtfully. That does not mean you cannot disagree, however. There are ways to disagree politely. If you have a different point of view, respect your parents or others enough to listen to what they have to say first. They will respect you for that. Once you've heard their side, tell them calmly how you feel or what you think. You might not get your own way, but they'll be more willing to listen. Eventually you will open better and better lines of communication, which will help get your message across.

Yelling to make your point never works.

Q. ***Why do I have to be quiet when my mom is on the telephone?***

A. If you're close enough to disturb the conversation she is having, you absolutely must be quiet. This is true when anybody is on the telephone. Respect the right of two people to speak privately, without interruption. The same rule applies to people who are talking face-to-face. Everyone has a right to privacy. Put yourself in their shoes. How would you feel if you were talking on the phone with a friend and your mom interrupted you?

Nobody looks good chewing gum.
Don't chew it in public.

Q. ***Are there any rules about chewing gum?***

A. Yes, there are. Don't chew gum where people gather to teach, talk, eat, or worship or in any place where noise and bubble snapping will create a distraction. Chewing gum while you're talking with someone on the telephone sounds like a firecracker going off in the listener's ear. In other words, just about the only time it is OK to chew gum is when you're by yourself or just hanging out with friends or family. Never chew when you're a guest in someone's home unless your host is also chewing gum and offers you some. And by all means, don't stick your gum under the table.

Remember to clean up
after yourself in the
kitchen and bathroom.

Q. ***My brother always leaves the bathroom a mess. The cap is off the toothpaste, a towel is rolled up into a ball on the floor, and there's water splashed everywhere. How can I get him to pay attention when I tell him how gross he is?***

A. Sadly, this is not behavior a person outgrows easily. A young slob just becomes an adult slob and continues to drive others up the wall with his or her behavior. Forget about telling him how gross he is. There are better ways of getting his attention: a direct threat, bribery with tickets to a sports event or rock concert, potential parental intervention. Here are some of the practical avenues you can take.

Be honest with yourself. Think about some of the things you do that drive him crazy. There must be some. Do you borrow a sweater or T-shirt and not tell him? You need to negotiate. Tell him if he cleans up after himself you'll promise to keep your hands off his stuff. This strategy requires two important things from you: first, keep your agreement; second, give him positive reinforcement such as "Thanks, the bathroom looks great these days." Not doing these things will result in failure. Dealing with a problem in the adult business world by negotiation is known as *compromise.* Once you master compromise, you'll find it a very useful skill. You can use it to solve far more complicated problems than keeping the bathroom clean.

Another practical method is to round up support from other family members. After all, your parents make the house rules. The problem with involving parents, however, is that you might get your way with the bathroom but lose your brother's willingness to help you in other ways unless he's forced to do so.

Finally, remember that the best way to teach anything is to set a good example.

Q. ***If I do something wrong, do I need to tell the truth about it?***

A. There isn't a person alive who hasn't made a mistake or done something wrong. Doing a wrong thing does not make a person bad. It just means he or she did something wrong. The difference between a person who respects himself and others and a person who doesn't care about himself or others is the ability to be honest about himself to others.

Being truthful means both telling the truth about yourself and your actions to other people and being truthful to yourself. For example, let's say you knocked over a lamp by accident and broke it. That could happen to anyone. In that case it would be important to tell the owner of the lamp what you did and offer to repair or replace it.

If, however, you deliberately knocked over the lamp because you were angry at the person who owned it, you must go one step further. You still must tell the owner and replace or repair the lamp. You also have to be honest with yourself and admit that you did a very spiteful and mean thing. Trying to tell yourself a lie or to convince yourself that it was a simple accident will only continue to eat at your conscience and rob you of your self-respect.

Q. ***When guests come to our house, what should I do?***

A. This is really simple. All you have to do is think how you would want to be treated if you were a guest in someone else's home. If you answer the door, greet your houseguests with a warm smile and a hello even if they're not there to see you. Welcome them inside. Invite them to sit down. Take their coats. Offer them something to drink, like water, tea, or soda. The hardest part might be making conversation if you're alone for a while. Just jump in and do it. Start by asking a straightforward question that will get them talking about themselves, like "What have you been doing this summer? Are you taking a vacation?" By that time the person they came to visit at your house should have appeared and you will have made the guests feel welcome and comfortable. That's the way you would like to be treated, isn't it?

Being neat and clean is more important than wearing the latest fashions.

Q. ***Why can't I wear sneakers with a suit?***

A. For the same reason you wouldn't want to wear a suit to play basketball: it doesn't get the job done. If you're going to play the game, it is important to wear the right uniform.

2
Manners and Etiquette in School

"Courtesy costs nothing. Manners make your fortune."
Proverb

For parents . . .

From age five to age eighteen, school becomes the most important stage of social interaction for most American children. The timing is terrible. On top of normal childhood fears, awkwardness, hormonal changes, and academic pressure, school years for the first time force children to deal with authority figures who are not parents and peers who are not siblings.

If ever knowledge of a code of social conduct would make life easier, these years are the time and school is the place.

Unfortunately, they don't teach etiquette in America's public schools. It is, I believe, a major omission of our educational system. Consider how life would improve for most students if that missing code of conduct were provided early in elementary school in an orderly and systematic fashion by someone other than nagging parents and via a textbook to give the code weight and authority.

Would school days be better if students were formally taught early on that it is wrong to interrupt when someone else is talking, or that it is right and expected to stop and help when another student has dropped books in the hallway, or that a beloved teacher deserves a letter of thanks at the end of the school year? I believe so, for these reasons:

Etiquette assumes a person innocent until proved guilty and, when a person is found guilty, also provides ways of dealing with that. Therefore, learning etiquette bestows acceptable methods for children to avoid confrontation and conflict. Etiquette sets down rules that always give others the benefit of a doubt, rules that permit others to correct themselves, rules that permit negotiation rather than resorting to a punch in the nose. For example, a child who knows to ask a question such as "Did you know this seating section is reserved for sixth-graders?" is far less likely to end up in trouble than a child who says "This is my seat. Get out." Call it what you will—manners, politeness, etiquette—but always call it a way to a more livable life.

Etiquette also teaches tolerance and compromise. These are essential life skill lessons. Adjusting to a school is akin to adjusting to a corporate culture later in life. Each school and the people in it, like each job environment and the workers in it, is different. Codes of conduct and formality change from school to school and job to job. If children learn early that the road to success is paved with rules of conduct—and it is important to pick up those rules quickly—they will move more smoothly through life.

Etiquette teaches the ability and confidence to adjust to change. It gives children a firm foundation on which to stand as the world swirls around them. Children who know the general rules about how to behave in any given situation will be able to alter and apply those rules as situations change. For example, I once taught in a private, inner-city ghetto school that, very much against the grain of the neighborhood, required students to wear uniforms—shirts, ties, sweaters, and black dress shoes instead of sneakers. When walking to school in uniform, these students often were taunted for the way they dressed by kids going to public school wearing the uniform of the streets. These students asked me what to do when confronted with these taunts. My answer was to carry their ties and black shoes in their bookbags until they got to the front door of the school, then change into uniform. They learned it was possible to adjust to satisfy both dress codes and avoid conflict.

Etiquette is one of the most effective forms of democracy. Etiquette is a great equalizer throughout a life span. There is no economic barrier to learning manners. The need for schooling in etiquette is universal, and the earlier, the better. In fact I've found that my students in underprivileged circumstances tend to soak up any information they can if it will help them get ahead. For example, in an eighth-grade ghetto school class I teach, a welcoming committee of five young men awaits my arrival at the door to escort me to class. One carries my books, another my coat, a third my umbrella. One leads; one brings up the rear. They vie for the chance to help me off with my coat. And when one day after class all five fumbled while trying to help me get the coat on, they rallied to my invitation for an impromptu lesson on helping with coats, yelled "Hey, cool!" and called to their classmates to join them for the lesson.

Finally, etiquette honors cultural diversity and customs. It permits children to speak in their own voices. For example, unless I carefully explain that every American greeting includes a handshake and direct eye contact, my Latin American students will be lost. Neither is part of their culture and, in fact, this greeting runs counter to everything they've been taught about greetings. Once they learn that cultural greetings differ, they adjust without embarrassment and use the proper method in the proper circumstance.

The etiquette lessons throughout this book are primarily American and should be recognized as such. They are not intended to invalidate the etiquette of other cultures. If your child attends a multicultural school, please remember this as you teach. It sometimes is a difficult lesson. Children are particularly susceptible to feeling like second-class citizens if their cultures are invalidated. I once taught a little girl who dejectedly told me one of my lessons got her into trouble at home. When she informed her parents that boys were supposed to stand when girls left or rejoined the dinner table, her father became angry and flatly refused to believe her. He was Chinese. That day I was the student.

For all these reasons, etiquette should become part of the curriculum in every school. Until that happens, however, it is still up to America's parents to fill the gap.

It probably has been a long time since you've been in school. It probably is difficult for you to remember the slights, embarrassments, annoyances, and blunders suffered there. The rest of this chapter may bring it all back. These questions were freshly written by children who are still suffering them today.

It often is more valuable to listen than to talk.

Bragging

Q. *One of the guys in my class brags all the time. How should I act around him?*

A. People who brag usually do it to cover up the fact that they really don't feel good about themselves. With this in mind, you could take pity on your classmate, but it still doesn't make it fun to be around him. On the positive side, you have been given a great gift. Now you know how boring it is to be around a person who talks only about himself. There are several ways you can act around him. You can try changing the subject when he starts talking, but this isn't easy. You can avoid him whenever possible. Or, if you are a true friend and value his friendship, you can take him aside and say something like "Hey, you're a great guy. We all know that, so you don't have to tell us yourself all the time." He should get the point.

Bullies

Q. *Some people in school call me bad names, but I don't want to tell on them. These people are mean. Sometimes they make fun of me or hit or kick me. I am tired of being treated this way. What should I do?*

A. You don't have to be treated that way, and you certainly should not be. Unfortunately, life is not always fair. The way you are being treated physically reminds me of a very popular movie where the main character had a problem fitting in. Daniel-san in *The Karate Kid* overcame his troubles with the help of a very wise teacher, some martial arts moves, and a Hollywood screenplay that, in the end, earned him respect and dignity.

Part of the essence of martial arts is knowing how to defend yourself but never using those methods as a weapon to hurt others. The bully, on the other hand, has no inner sense of security or inner value to rely on. Bullies strike out to control people by making them afraid. Making others fearful is the bully's only ticket to acceptance by you and the rest of your schoolmates. Bullies really have no friends.

Although learning the martial arts is valuable for anybody as a tool for living, you don't have to be Bruce Lee to handle the bullies in your life. The key is to learn how to be above your tormentors. To do that, you must realize and remember that what they say and do is their problem. After all, this certainly is a clique or group that you don't need to be accepted by. I'm sure there are others in your class who feel the same way. Those are the people you want for friends.

Practically speaking, there is absolutely no reason to tolerate physical abuse. Ask for help. Tell your parents first and don't be afraid to tell your teacher. I'll bet those bullies are counting on the fact that they've scared you out of telling. But remember, telling your parents and teachers will gain you only limited protection. True, lasting protection comes from believing in yourself, respecting others, and choosing your friends well. Spend your time and energy learning all about things that interest you. Be the very best person you can be. The more self-confident you become, the smaller the bullies will seem to you.

One last note: no matter how old you get, there always will be bullies in your life. You can choose whether you'll let them help you grow or whether they will stunt your growth. Each bully is an opportunity to become stronger and more successful. After a while we come to recognize that, if it weren't for bullies, we probably would have been lazy and content—and that's how a person gets old before his time.

Don't be embarrassed to admit you don't know the answer.

Cheating

Q. ***There's a person in our class who cheats on tests by looking at other people's papers. We don't want to rat him out, but what should we do?***

A. This is a tough one. All of us get the opportunity to deal with something like this sooner or later. It never gets easier.

The sad truth is that the only person the cheater really hurts is himself. He loses friends, trust, self-respect, and, ultimately, self-confidence. For these reasons doing the right thing here is a very delicate matter. You may be able to solve the problem without ratting him out.

First, cover your test paper as you take the test. That will send a clear message that you're onto his game, you don't approve of cheating, and you're not willing to help him keep it up any longer. You won't need to say a word.

Wait and see what happens on the next test. If it happens again, continue to shield your answers and speak to him alone about his cheating afterward. Say something like "Look, cut out trying to crib from my test papers. You know what you're doing is wrong. Others have noticed, too." If this fails, you might consider asking a group of classmates who also have had the same problem with him to confront him together. If it comes to that, be careful. Be calm and respectful so as not to create a public humiliation. That would solve nothing. No raised voices. No name calling. No "holier than thou" preaching.

Choose one person to speak and lay out the facts. Tell him his behavior is basically stealing, that it is wrong, that it is not fair to those of you who have studied and prepared for the test, and that you won't tolerate his cheating anymore.

He may assume that you all will tell school authorities, but you don't have to threaten that. All you have to do is stick to your guns and cover your papers. That should solve the problem. Telling your teacher is an option, but you'll probably respect yourselves a lot more if you handle this situation yourselves. After the episode is over, put it behind you. Your friend will have a tough enough time looking you all in the eye every day. There will be no need for any other reminder of his dishonest behavior. Everybody deserves a second chance.

Dances

Q. ***Sixth-graders are allowed to go to school dances for the first time this year. Is it OK for a girl to ask a boy to dance?***

A. If the world waited for boys to do everything, only half would get done. Although it was the custom in the past for guys to ask first for the favor of a dance, times have changed. That's good for everybody. It is perfectly acceptable today for a girl to ask a boy to dance. Girls also can ask boys for dates these days. Ever since women entered the work force in major numbers, women have been demanding and receiving the same choices and opportunities men always enjoyed. The days when you had to be a wilting, helpless wallflower are gone. Remember that many guys are just as unsure of themselves as you are. They probably will feel greatly relieved if the pressure of "asking first" didn't fall only to them.

Baseball caps come off indoors,
whether at home or at school.

Hats

Q. ***Why can't you wear hats in school?***

A. Because your school has a roof and heat, that's why. Hats are meant to protect you from the sun or cold. There is no practical or logical reason to wear them indoors. Etiquette rules do change with time, however, so hang on to your hat. In another fifty years you may be in luck.

Hazing

Q. ***When you were in school, what was the rudest thing students did?***

A. Make fun of people for things they couldn't help, like being short or tall. I was the tallest girl in my class, I wore braces and glasses, and I was a very good student. My classmates labeled me a "brain," teased me all the time for being tall and funny-looking, and never really took the time to learn about me as a person. That was a while ago, but I still think that mean-spirited teasing is the rudest, cruelest thing anybody can do.

There are plenty of things to learn . . . even when school is out.

Q. ***I'm in the fifth grade. In our middle school, eighth-graders make fifth-graders carry their books, give them their seats on the bus and in the cafeteria, and other things just because we're younger. I don't think this is right or polite. Is it?***

A. No, it isn't. But it is a fact of life. As long as the treatment isn't mean-spirited (you know what I mean; nasty threats from bullies and the like), don't lose your sense of humor and go along with it. Remember that eighth-graders were in the fifth grade once, too. They probably put up with the custom. That's probably how they learned it.

It may seem light-years away at the moment, but before long you'll be in eighth grade, and you'll have your turn. I know that doesn't help the way you feel now, but the best way to make this stop is to be good-natured even if this teasing makes you angry. When the older kids think you're bothered, they'll just turn up the heat to get more of a reaction out of you. And I wonder whether, when you are in eighth grade, your experience will make you treat fifth-graders the way you want to be treated now.

Thank the driver when you get off the bus.

Q. ***On my school bus a lot of people make fun of one girl because she looks different. She ignores them, but they don't stop. I don't think this is right, but I'm just one person. What can I do?***

A. Can one person speak up and make a difference? Absolutely. Will the group most likely make fun of you when you speak up? Probably. But don't be ashamed. Instead, be proud of doing the right thing. In the long run, standing up to such people will gain you respect from the group and loyalty from the victim you're defending.

Usually the kind of cruelty you describe is fueled by one or two bullies who dominate by making others fear they won't be approved by them. Chances are good that you're not the only person on the bus who feels this taunting is wrong. By speaking up, you may get some unexpected help to stop it. Just say something like "Leave her alone. How would you like everybody to make fun of you that way?" You won't have to sound angry, scream, or use force to make your point.

As uncomfortable as you may feel about doing this, you will be in impressive company. Think of how much all of us have gained because people such as Abraham Lincoln, the Reverend Dr. Martin Luther King, Jr., and Mother Teresa spoke out or acted when they saw other human beings being treated unfairly.

Swinging quickly when wearing a backpack or book bag can injure those behind you or cause damage. Be careful.

Helping

Q. ***A girl in my school dropped all of her books and paper all over the hall. I stopped to help her pick them up. The other guys made fun of me. Did I do the right thing?***

A. Absolutely. Whoever needs help should get help. It doesn't matter whether it is a girl or a guy helping or being helped. I'll bet if you had stopped to help another guy, the rest of them never would have noticed. Congratulations. You set a great example.

Listen to the answer after you have asked the question.

Q. ***My mom says that at school I should give up my place in line at the water fountain to a girl if she's behind me. Why do I have to? We have only a couple of minutes between classes.***

A. It is a kindness to allow anyone to get help before you. If a schoolmate—guy or girl—seems much thirstier than you or perhaps looks very hot or needs to take some medication, it is a nice gesture to give up your place in line. However, there is no special reason to just because the person behind you is female. If girls can ask for dates and enjoy some of the other choices that guys have, they can't expect special treatment because they're female. Girls can't have it both ways.

Never push your way on to or off of the school bus.

Introductions

Q. ***How do I introduce my mother to my new teacher and friends?***

A. Adults have a tough time with this, too. It is confusing to know which name to say first. The most important thing to remember about introductions is to actually make them, instead of avoiding them because you're afraid to make a mistake.

The correct way to introduce your mother to your teacher is to say "Ms. Lammers, I'd like to introduce my mom, Mrs. Brackup."

The correct way to introduce your friends to your mother is to say: "Mom, this is my friend Frank Hales. He sits behind me in school, and we're in the Glee Club together. Frank, this is my mother, Mrs. Brackup."

It helps to give a little information about the people you are introducing so that they will have something to talk about. Don't forget to say your mother's last name, especially if it is different from yours.

A good way to remember which name to use first in an introduction is that "the biggest star gets top billing." That means you would introduce a younger person to an older person, like: "Mom, I'd like to introduce Frank's twin sister, Sharon."

Introduce a nondignitary to a dignitary, like "Congressman Smith, I'd like to introduce my father, Dr. Brackup." A dignitary would be an elected official or a religious official. We give these persons this respect because we respect the offices they hold. It does *not* mean that, as people, they are better or more important than anyone else.

Everybody gets befuddled making introductions. If you get all tongue-tied, just say "Ms. Lammers, this is Dr. Brackup." Don't worry about which name goes first. Go for it. Everybody will appreciate your effort.

Invitations

Q. ***My mom said I could have a sleep-over party but that I could invite only ten girls. What do I say to the other girls in my class if they ask me why they weren't invited?***

A. Nobody likes to feel left out. Ask your mother if you can have another party sometime later if this one works out. That way you can truthfully say your mom limited the number of guests to ten but you are hoping to have another sleep-over later in the year for the rest of your friends. Build your guest list around an interest that all those invited share; for example, all the girls who are in the same club or on the same team. Everyone will understand how your invitations were made, and you probably won't hurt anybody's feelings. People who aren't interested in the same thing probably won't want to spend a whole night talking about stuff that might bore them but amuse the rest of the group.

Lunch

Q. ***Sometimes kids in my class want me to share my lunch with them when they have their own. What should I do?***

A. You're not obligated to share your food with someone who has plenty. A polite "You have your own lunch. This is just enough for me" will do. If you have more food than you need or somebody would go hungry without your help, by all means share. But if someone is just bullying you to get your lunch, tell your teacher or your parents.

Q. ***Sometimes kids in my class say my lunch looks yucky. What should I do?***

A. Calling someone's lunch "yucky" certainly isn't a very kind thing to do. The important thing is, does it look and taste yucky to you, or are these people just teasing you? It is true that some food tastes great but looks grim. My advice is that if your food tastes good to you, be an individual and let those comments roll off your back. Those are pretty dumb remarks. I don't think they are worth your losing out on a tasty lunch, do you?

Make friends with the new person in your class.

New School

Q. ***I just came to a new school. How do I make friends?***

A. Sometimes when we change schools or neighborhoods, it feels like we've been transported to a planet full of aliens. It feels like we're either being watched constantly or being ignored. It can seem like a bad dream, and we can't wake up. I know. I've changed schools, neighborhoods, and even countries many times. Here are some things you can do to get to know your classmates and help you become friends with them.

The most important tip I can give you is to pay attention to your classmates instead of feeling uneasy because you don't know them. That way you'll discover which of them seem to share your interests in school subjects, sports, and other activities. It will help provide you with things to talk about, too. For example, you can say something like "I'm Jerome Burton, and I just started at this school. I noticed that you really seem to like math class. So do I. What other kinds of things do you like to do?" Then pay close attention to the answer.

Remember that paying attention to them and noticing the kinds of things that appear to be important to them always makes people feel good. When people feel you're interested in them, they become interested in you.

I'm sure you've thought of joining extracurricular activities to get into the mainstream of activity at school. No doubt there are clubs and teams to join. Be sure to investigate all the possibilities.

Don't be afraid to ask your teacher to help you. Sometimes adults get so wound up in their jobs that they don't see a situation right under their noses. Your teacher might think that you've already made friends.

Remember too that many a star got there by being a humble volunteer first. Don't shy away from opportunities to help out. Is there a job that isn't getting done around school because nobody is willing to be responsible for it? Never be afraid to serve. It is a great way to bolster your own self-respect and earn the respect of others. Another avenue to meet new friends is a church or other place of worship, if you attend one regularly. Most have a number of activities for young people.

Although I'm sure right now you're feeling challenged about becoming part of your new community, once you conquer your apprehension and move forward, you will have learned one of life's most valuable lessons. Go for it.

Punishment

Q. ***What do I do if I get hollered at for something I didn't do?***

A. How you act depends on where you are when it happens. At home with your parents, it would be all right to protest and try to set the record straight. At school or in other public settings, remember that two wrongs don't make a right. If you're being blamed in front of other people for something you didn't do, don't make matters worse by arguing with your teacher. It will only embarrass everybody. Talk in private afterward. If you really weren't at fault, it becomes the accuser's responsibility to set the record straight—in public.

Responsibility

Q. ***I am in fifth grade. Lately it seems some students in my class (myself included) are having trouble understanding what it means to be responsible. What would you consider the duties of a fifth-grader, and how can we show more responsibility?***

A. I really believe the duties of a fifth-grader are basically the same as for an adult. Life gets more complicated as we get older, but being responsible is pretty much the same for all of us. You asked for my personal opinion, so here is what "being responsible" means to me.

It first means recognizing that I am a child of my Creator or God. When I feel mean or nasty, I have to stop myself and remember that the greater part of me was not born mean and nasty.

Being responsible also means being true to myself—staying healthy, keeping fit, telling the truth to myself and to others. It means not breaking my word, doing what I say I will, and being willing to admit when I'm wrong. It means being willing to laugh at myself when I do goofy things.

Responsibility means I have to try to be the best person I can be and not be too hard on myself when I slip up. It means respecting and honoring members of my family, even when it is hard and I don't agree with them. It means supporting and sticking by my friends and being willing to share my ups and downs with them.

Basically, being responsible means accepting whatever responsibilities are there for me—my marriage and my job—and treating all people in my life with as much kindness, dignity, and respect as I would like them to give me. Thank you for asking the question. It really made me think.

Spitting

Q. ***When and where should you spit in school?***

A. The only truly acceptable time to spit is in the dentist's chair when instructed to do so. Trust me. You can distinguish yourself as a nasty geek if you go around spitting. Think about the picture that comes to mind when you hear the phrase *spitting mad.* Not pretty. If you absolutely must spit, excuse yourself from class or the dining table and use the bathroom in private. Be sure it's clean when you leave.

Teachers

Q. ***My teacher pronounces my name wrong. How can I tell her the right way? She hasn't asked for help.***

A. Teachers are human, too (although you may not think so at times). It is bad manners to correct someone in public, so don't roll your eyes or make faces to the class when she does it. Instead, ask to see her for a moment alone before or after class. Tell her then how your family pronounces your name. She is sure to appreciate your concern and good manners, because nobody—especially a person in authority—likes to be corrected in front of other people. On the other hand, if you happen to be at a party and new friends mispronounce your name, it is fine to tell them the correct way at that time, as long as you don't do it angrily.

Q. ***Should our class get our teacher a gift for her birthday or Christmas?***

A. Great idea, but there are some important things to remember. The gift should not be extravagant. It should be something everyone in the class can contribute to without financial hardship. Be sensitive to this. Don't embarrass anyone who might not be able to afford to give money.

Super gifts for teachers can be plants, a tape or CD, or nice chocolates, for example. You'll need to be organized. Form a small committee of volunteers to decide what you're going to give; how much the present should cost; how you're going to collect, keep track of, and handle the money; who will actually purchase the gift; who will wrap it; and how and when you'll present it. Don't forget to buy a card and get everybody to sign it. Better still, make the card.

There are creative ways to include classmates who cannot afford to contribute money. To be part of the gift-giving process, they can wrap the present or be the ones responsible for purchasing it or for getting everyone to sign the card.

Another, and perhaps better, idea is to make something for your teacher yourselves. In my view something the class makes as a gift would be treasured by any teacher. Everyone can be included. The very best gift you can give is your time and attention. What about making a poster with a class picture on it, signed and framed? How about writing and singing a class song for your teacher? The best surprise gift I ever received was a series of rap songs about manners that one eighth-grade class wrote and performed for me. I framed them and put them on my office wall where I can see them every day.

Q. ***In gym the teacher makes us choose up sides for dodge ball. The same people are always picked last. Isn't there a more fair way to do this? I always get picked last, and I feel like a loser before the game begins.***

A. Have you talked with your teacher? You should. Perhaps there are several simple, easy, and fair ways to remedy this situation. For example, have a rotating captain system. There would be a different captain for each game, and those captains get to choose their own players. That way the same people will not always be chosen last. You also could suggest a lottery. Let's say there are twelve players, making two teams of six. We'll call them red team and green team. Make up twelve chits, six red and six green, and draw them out of a hat. This method leaves player selection totally to chance, and nobody gets their feelings hurt.

Uniforms

Q. ***My school has a dress code. All the girls wear uniform skirts. Some of the guys think it's funny to stand under the stairs and look up our skirts when we walk to the next floor. What is the best way to get them to stop?***

A. I think you should wear boxer shorts—and the wilder, the better. Girls and guys have been going through this kind of thing since girls first wore skirts above the ankle. Let's be practical. You can't refuse to go up the stairs, and I doubt that your school will install elevators or make the stairwells boy-free to accommodate you and your friends. What the guys really want to see is the expression on your face. You can't drop books or water balloons on their heads (although it might be tempting). Boys will go to great lengths to see if they can reduce girls to a state of helplessness. They want you to blush, shriek, and giggle. Don't do it. A better strategy is to outsmart them at their own game. Ignore them, especially if all the girls can do that together. Remember, it is your reaction to what they're doing that makes the stairwell game appealing. Once you and your friends refuse to play their game, there is no game. The guys will become bored and give it up. If they don't give up, you should tell your teacher the problem and ask for help.

Q. ***At my new school we have to wear uniforms. I don't like the way they look. I hate wearing them. Why do we have to wear uniforms?***

A. In a sense we all wear uniforms. A businessperson, a lawyer, or an accountant usually wears a suit. An athlete wears sweats for practice and a uniform on the field. A construction worker most likely wears heavy boots and a hard hat. These uniforms are partly chosen for their function—the right equipment for the right job—and partly according to what the leaders of the organization think will make its workers reliable, capable, efficient, and safe.

Most formal uniforms, such as military uniforms or a nurse's outfit, are a combination of form and function. Uniforms are a way to identify people for what they do. Think of how confusing it would be if you went to a restaurant and the serving staff didn't wear uniforms. You would never know who was supposed to take your order, who should direct you to your seat, or who would clear the table. If you look at a server's uniform in a restaurant, you probably will see that it is comfortable, easy to move around in, made of strong fabric, easily laundered, and, in general, flattering to any wearer.

The same is true of your school uniform. There are several practical reasons your school insists on a uniform. It probably looks good, or at the very least appropriate, for every function, whether in school or at a class outing. It makes it easy for you to spot other members of your group. Although it may not be flashy, it probably is comfortable indoors and out. It is easy to move around in so that, in case of an emergency, constricting or loose clothing would not cause a safety problem. It probably is affordable to everybody. It is democratic in that it eliminates worry for those who don't have the money for fashionable new styles and therefore doesn't discriminate, prevents "clothing cliques," and encourages a team spirit. Finally, it probably is very easy to care for.

I would never try to convince you to love your uniform. I felt the same way about mine when I was in school. Understanding why uniforms are practical, however, may help you tolerate them more cheerfully. Besides, there are other, more constructive ways to express your individuality and taste than to worry about a situation you can't change.

3
Between the Sexes

"Good manners is the blossom of good sense."
Proverb

For parents . . .

Proper conduct between the sexes often remains a puzzle even to those of us who have had years of practice. You can only imagine how difficult it must be for children and teenagers today. No area of etiquette is changing faster. The rules of chivalry, the original standards, have been modified or cast aside. What once was "polite" might now be considered insulting. What once seemed like common sense may no longer be relevant. What to do, what to do?

The old rules of chivalry, which governed how men and women treated each other for several centuries, called for deference by virtue of gender, age, and social caste. In that model gentlemen called on ladies, gentlemen never extended a hand to a lady first, gentlemen held doors and chairs, gentlemen stood when a lady entered or departed a room, castes were openly acknowledged with subservient actions, and so forth. These rules were based on perceived weaknesses by sex or superiority by birth and rank. It is for the better that they are changing, particularly for women and minorities.

The shift in America began thirty to forty years ago. Women, perceived as weak under the rules of chivalry, entered the workforce in numbers that continue to increase today and proved their strength. Minorities, treated as inferior castes under the chivalry system, demanded and received equal rights and proved their equality. Today, racial, cultural, and sexual diversity is entrenched in the workplace. All sectors play strong decision-making roles in American corporate culture, economy, and government.

These new decision-making groups exerted their power largely through America's corporate culture. Corporate culture has long had its own set of etiquette rules. Those rules are based on deference according to corporate "rank," much like any military system. Therefore, as more parents of both sexes and from all sub-groups entered the corporate culture, they absorbed this militarylike system of etiquette. Naturally their children learned far more of these corporate attitudes and manners than those based on chivalry. The result is that chivalry has faded and corporate etiquette has emerged as the dominant force governing modern American interpersonal relationships.

The effect of this shift on relations between the sexes has been dramatic and confusing. For example, young girls may now ask young boys for dates. They see their peers doing it. At the same time, their parents may disagree and give conflicting signals. Thus the older chivalrous tradition confuses and haunts these budding and already-difficult relationships.

This chapter attempts to sort new from outmoded, impractical from sensible. The lessons should be especially useful in helping your children deal with emotionally loaded questions, like "Can I ask a boy to dance?"

The essence of most questions children and teens will ask about their encounters with the opposite sex will have something to do with the nature of relationships. They may ask about the rules, but they're really wondering about the mystery. After all, to youngsters it often seems that there are two distinct species of humans on earth. The opposite sex acts, speaks, and dresses differently, is interested in different things, and relates to his or her same-sex friends differently. At some point your child will want to know how to bridge this gap. At that time you may want to take an inventory of your own successful relationships to determine what made them work. I believe you'll find that those good relationships are based on being kind to each other and anticipating each other's needs in almost any situation. These, after all, are the building blocks of etiquette.

Here are some elements that make relationships between people of any age work. You can tell your child to use some or all of these points as guidelines when attempting to sort out those mysterious feelings.

Honesty: Can you be truthful? Can you "be yourself?" A good relationship cannot be built on lies. Honesty includes being honest with yourself. For example, do you really like smoking cigarettes, or are you just doing it because your partner does? Do you really want to be on the football team, or are you doing it because it will make your father happy? Do you really like the class celebrity as a person, or do you want to hang out together because it will make you more popular? Are you being you or just putting up a front to make someone else like you? If you can't be honest with yourself, you can't be honest with the other person in a relationship.

Support: Do you support and praise each other? Remember, support doesn't necessarily mean you have to agree all the time. In fact it means letting each other know how you honestly feel. Players on great sports teams don't always agree on the next move, but once the decision is made, they honor and back it 100 percent. Just believing that the other person on your team is great isn't enough. You have to tell each other.

Friends: Are you the other person's best friend? Do you show that you are listening and trying to understand his or her feelings? Never dismiss the feelings of a friend as silly or unimportant.

Faithfulness: Do you stick by each other when disappointments arise? Do you try your best to see disappointments through the other person's eyes? For example, you may not care about basketball, but your partner does. When he or she doesn't make the team and feels like the world's biggest loser, are you there for support even though you may not understand what the big deal is?

Punctuality: Are you where you say you'll be on time? The best way to make others crazy, and prove you don't care about their feelings, is to keep them waiting.

Keeping Your Word: Do you stand by the agreements you make? If you make a promise, do you keep it? Can you keep the promises in your relationship because you want to and not because you feel obligated?

Respect for Others: Do you both respect the important people in each other's life? Even if you'd rather be bitten by a rattlesnake than go to your friend's parents' house for dinner, do you still go and act politely? And even if the food tastes like old shoes and the conversation at dinner is as exciting as watching grass grow, do you compromise graciously and never complain afterward?

Fun: Can you have fun together? Do you laugh a lot together? All of us feel like little kids at times. We need to be able to let go and be silly. Shared laughter is a sign of an easy relationship.

Giving Space: Are you able to accept that the other person has his or her own life? Don't be upset when the other person needs time alone. And don't be afraid to speak up when you do. Possessiveness is unnecessary in a healthy relationship.

Those are the general road signs on the way to a good relationship. Now here are the questions asked by boys and girls embarking on their first relationships with the opposite sex.

Asking for a Date

Q. ***How do I ask for a date? I feel really stupid, and I get tongue-tied, so I chicken out.***

A. Whether it is a guy asking a girl or a girl asking a guy, the rules are the same:

1. An invitation for a date shouldn't be unexpected. Are you at least friendly acquaintances? Both of you should, at the very least, have positive, friendly feelings for each other. If you don't have some familiarity with each other, hold off on asking for a date and get to know this person better on a casual level. Make a point to hang around together, talk easily, and find out if you share any interests. If all goes well . . .
2. Decide what the date will be. Keep in mind that it is important to try to please the person you're inviting. By now you should know what interests you share. For example, an invitation to a ballet probably won't hold much appeal for a die-hard sports fan who would rather watch a football game. First dates should be easy and casual for both people. Don't try to make it a big, special event that causes nervousness. Keep the cost

modest so that reciprocating, if it comes to a second date, won't be difficult.

3. Ask for the date face-to-face or by telephone. Give plenty of advance notice. At least four days is a good guideline. Spur-of-the-moment invitations can seem insulting.
4. Be specific. Make it plain that you're asking for a date for a certain place, time, and event. You can say something like "Would you like to go to the new Star Trek movie with me on Saturday afternoon? I can meet you outside the theater at 4:00 P.M." Do not say something like "Let's go to the movies sometime" and expect it to turn into a date.
5. If the answer is yes, it is up to you to take care of the details. Get to the theater early and buy the tickets, for example. Usually the person who does the asking also pays. Don't expect your date to split expenses if you haven't worked that out together in advance.
6. If the answer is no, listen for verbal clues to whether you should ask again at a later date. You should be able to tell if there truly is a conflicting reason this person can't go with you on that day and time or whether you're just wasting your time. If the turndown doesn't sound like it was meant to be forever, don't be afraid to say you would like to invite this person out again later. Then observe how this person treats you and choose whether to extend a second invitation.

Breaking Up

Q. ***I've been going steady for three months, and I want to break up. The problem is that I really like my boyfriend's best friend and want to go out with him. What should I do?***

A. The romantic triangle. It is a problem that has dominated literature through the ages. You are in famous company. What you need to do is fairly simple but not easy. If you search your innermost feelings, I think you'll probably find that something is missing from your relationship with your boyfriend. If that was not the case, any other fellow would not attract you. The lesson here is: don't make your boyfriend's best friend the issue. He probably isn't.

You must deal with your boyfriend honestly, openly, and directly. That means face-to-face. Spare him the details of your wandering eye. Above all, spare him all details of what he did, or did not do, to lose you. Your goal is to have a clean break and as polite and kind a relationship afterward as possible. Don't waste time trying to find "the right opportunity" to talk. The problem will only get worse in your mind, and he surely will sense that something is wrong. That's when senseless, hurtful fights occur. Neither of you needs that.

Say something like "I've been thinking about it, and I'd like to go out with other people. Maybe you should, too." Think about how you would feel if the shoe were on the other foot: Rejected? Hurt? Angry? You bet. He might react badly and, out of frustration, try to start a fight. Do your best to stay calm. Refuse to let him goad you into arguing. You don't have to give him reasons for your decision, but if you do, leave his friend out of it. That would be humiliating to him.

After you've broken up, treat him with respect. Be very careful never to say anything nasty or hurtful about him to anyone. As for his friend, avoid beating a path to his door immediately. Once the dust settles and you're back in circulation, he will know about it and let you know whether he is interested in going out with you. You should consider that perhaps he is not interested in you. He might feel a sense of loyalty to his friend (which would be natural and honorable) and avoid dating you until his friend's spirits and social life are happier.

During this transition time you should give some serious thought to the whole concept of "going steady," which led you into this problem. It can make you feel secure and attractive, but it also is limiting to your social life, can become boring, and can also cause pressure between you and your partner. Perhaps you should decide to put off such commitments for a while and enjoy a more casual social life.

Whatever you decide, your dilemma is a perfect example of how, although we cannot control how we feel, we can control what we do about it. If you handle this situation respectfully, you set a standard for how you want and expect to be treated by others. Doing it correctly will earn the respect and admiration of others.

Words can hurt as much as punches. Watch what you say.

Q. ***My boyfriend dumped me. I'm really mad about it. How can I make him sorry?***

A. Cool off. I know . . . that's easier said than done and easy for me to say, right? But there is an old expression that goes something like "Living well is the best revenge." Think about the wisdom in that saying. Are you really sure you want to counterattack? Do you really think it will do any good? What if it backfires? Will other guys want to date you if you put all your energy into bad-mouthing your ex-boyfriend? Don't you think they'll be wondering how you will react if you disagree with them, too?

Be careful about what you say and to whom. Even if your ex-boyfriend acted like the most despicable rat in the universe, he won't need you to advertise it. People will figure it out for themselves. If you say or do things just to hurt him, he wins. You look bad.

So clench your teeth and find something else to do—play table tennis, run, help someone less fortunate than yourself, paint, write, anything to channel your anger elsewhere.

Instead of looking angry and hurt, accentuate the positive in yourself. Look your best. Be upbeat when you talk with friends. Don't complain about all the gory details of your failed romance, which will hurt, not help, your chances of getting back into circulation. Even if friends bait you (and they will) to say bad things about him, resist the temptation. Be active. Don't isolate yourself. That doesn't mean jumping into a new relationship right away. It just means that you should keep your eyes open for new choices in friends, new places to go, new people to meet, and new things to experience.

You can't pretend he never existed. The fact is that you've been handed a loss and it hurts. You're entitled to cry, to feel sad, to let it out, so don't try to stop that. Then pamper yourself. Take a long bubble bath. Buy new cosmetics or new clothes. And then go out and face the world and behave in ways that demonstrate the respect you once had for your ex-boyfriend that also will demonstrate the respect you have for yourself. The faster you reenter the social world—looking great and sounding upbeat—the faster you'll be able to put this behind you and get on with new and better relationships.

Dating and Parents

Q. ***If a guy asks you out and you are not allowed to date yet, what should you do?***

A. Tell the truth and don't be embarrassed or ashamed. We all have to live by rules that we don't like at one time or another. The good news is that when you decline the invitation you really are not rejecting him as a person. Be sure to be clear about your reasons for turning him down. Just say something like "Thanks a lot for inviting me. I'd love to go, but my parents don't allow me to date yet." I encourage you to be as matter-of-fact as you can. That way he will get the message that the decision is really beyond your control. At the same time, you won't be dishonoring or criticizing your parents. If this is somebody you would like to date, perhaps there are some group activities where you can spend time together—like school sports events, cultural events, or even parties. It is fine to seek out those opportunities as long as both of you know the ground rules and stick to them.

Q. ***I never know what to do when a date comes to pick me up at home. How do I introduce him to my parents?***

A. Nobody likes to feel helpless when meeting new people for the first time—not even parents. It is a good idea to fill your parents in on your date in advance so they'll have something to talk about. When your date calls, answer the door yourself and invite him in. Lead him to your parents and say, "Mom, Dad, this is David Smith. We know each other because we're in the same history class" or "David is on the school soccer team."

The idea here is to give your parents some information to work with in starting a conversation easily. Pronounce your date's first and last names clearly. Introduce your parents by their last names, as in "Mr. and Mrs. Jones."

Above all, don't disappear out the door before everybody has a few minutes to chat and get to know each other. A few extra minutes spent in conversation will put your parents at ease and make you look self-confident, too. This short conversation also will give you the opportunity to see how your date handles himself around adults. It might not be really important right now, but it will be important later.

Gifts

Q. ***My boyfriend is constantly giving me presents. First it was stuffed animals. Then it was books. About a week ago he gave me an expensive CD. His parents joke that he spends all his money on me. I would love to reciprocate, but he holds a job and gets an allowance, and I don't. I have gotten him a few gifts, but nowhere near the amount he's given me. I just don't feel comfortable being constantly bombarded by presents, either. What should I do?***

A. While most people would love to be in your situation, I can understand how you might feel smothered. You have a tightrope to walk, balancing between being considerate of his feelings and maintaining your own boundaries for what's appropriate and acceptable conduct in this relationship.

Instead of keeping score on who gives how many of what and at what price, why not deal with the central issue? It seems to me that sincere presents should please, not embarrass, the person they're given to. Instead of reluctantly accepting your boyfriend's gifts and then feeling uncomfortable, tell him kindly but firmly that you no longer can accept presents because they are getting in the way of your relationship. Together, set some ground rules, such as "presents are off-limits except for birthdays and major holidays, like Christmas." When he sees and understands how important this is to you, he should surely agree.

But don't be surprised if he breaks the rules at first. That's when the real challenge comes in, because you cannot accept the gift, whatever it is. Simply say something like "This is a wonderful gift, but I cannot accept it. We agreed. Remember?" If he argues that he'll be stuck with a book or sweater or anything else he selected "just for you," you must stand firm and recognize that it's his problem, not yours. It also will give you an opportunity to look at how he keeps his agreements, an element essential to any good relationship. It is easy to keep agreements we like. The true test of respect for another is keeping agreements out of honor and respect—even when they don't please us.

Say thank you and smile when someone compliments you.

Interest Signs

Q. ***What are some things boys say or do to let girls know they like them?***

A. Boys are strange creatures when it comes to communicating how they feel, especially to girls. It seems they are dedicated to pestering sisters and to confusing female friends. Don't expect common sense to help you figure it out in most cases. It doesn't work. It is a rare fellow indeed who actually will send you a letter or note expressing his feelings. Rarer still is the guy who will tell you face-to-face how he feels. That means you must develop your antennae to pick up the less-than-obvious clues. Here are some signals:

- consistent teasing, even to the point of making you get angry
- acting really weird or loud when you're around
- slapping you on the back as if you are one of the guys
- sweeping up from behind to pick you up in the middle of the hall at school

As bizarre as this kind of behavior might seem, it can be a sign of affection. What's really happening is that he wants to get your attention and just doesn't know how. So be kind in your thinking about these awkward demonstrations. And don't get too frustrated or irritated. The truth is that learning to interpret these signals can be a lifelong study. Just look at how many books and magazine articles have been devoted to it.

Liking Someone

Q. ***When will boys start liking me or asking me on dates? All of my friends keep talking about their dates, and I feel very embarrassed because I don't have any.***

A. Whether they're thirteen or thirty-five, boys are strange creatures. It is tough to predict what they're thinking or feeling, so you will waste a lot of time trying to anticipate their actions. The good news is, unlike times gone by, a girl quite properly can initiate a friendship with a boy. There is no reason to be afraid to say hello to someone you would like to know better, especially if he's in your school or a friend of someone you know.

It is important to try always to look your best. Well-groomed hair, skin, nails, teeth, and clothing are a must. If you are friendly and pleasant to everyone, you certainly don't run the risk of having one certain boy think you are crazy about him, and you won't get teased. Maybe you can arrange for a friend to have a small party and invite the boy you're interested in. When a boy talks to you, be interested in what he says (good advice when listening to anybody), but make sure he is interested in what you have to say as well. If he grunts or mumbles one-word answers to your questions or if he doesn't seem to pay attention, you may decide to set your sights elsewhere.

Go ahead and say something like "I'm going to the movies Saturday afternoon. Would you like to come along?" Let's face it. Inviting someone to anything is scary because we're afraid they'll say no. Boys feel the same way, but for centuries the pressure has been on them to do the asking. You might feel shy and unsure of yourself, but be careful that you don't let anyone misinterpret such behavior as aloofness. That's why it is so important to be pleasant and friendly to everyone.

Nobody invited me to my junior prom, and I was crushed. The day after the dance, one of the guys in my class asked me why I wasn't there. When I told him nobody had asked me, he said he was surprised and said that the guys had figured I must have had a date, so nobody had ever talked about it with me. Looking back, I think I should have asked one of the guys who he was taking. He probably then would have asked me who I was going with, and things might have worked out differently. I missed an important memory because I was too scared to speak up and admit that I could have used some help. I hope you can learn from my mistake.

Q. ***I like this one boy, but I don't know if he likes me. We hang around with each other, but I still want to know how to tell him I like him and how to tell if he likes me.***

A. There is one surefire way to get what you want here: ask for it. However, asking somebody of the opposite sex if you're special can be really uncomfortable and difficult to put into words effectively. In fact it can be downright scary. In my experience being simple, honest, direct, and light is a good way to do it. Keep your sense of humor. When you have an opportunity to be together and to talk easily with him, say something open like "I think you're special, and I like you more than a buddy. I really like hanging out with you." Keep in mind that boys are not exactly cool and suave when they're teenagers (and often as adults for that matter) so don't be surprised if he gets tongue-tied and fidgety. You may not get an answer then and there, but eventually you will.

Other Cultures

Q. ***There's a boy in my class who just moved here from Brazil. He's very nice, and I like him, but whenever we talk, he keeps moving closer and closer, which makes me feel really funny. What should I do?***

A. Because your friend is Latin-American, I suspect the situation you describe is simply cross-cultural. Every culture has its own "personal space" line. Some are closer than others. For example, an American would be uncomfortable and feel invaded if someone stood closer than an arm's length away. Orientals, especially Japanese, stand even farther away. Latinos and Middle Easterners stand much, much closer than Americans. In their own countries you can see them standing literally toe-to-toe. They may even touch each other with a hand on an elbow or a finger on a lapel.

Only you can decide whether your friend's behavior is sexually intimidating. It seems by the tone of your question that it isn't. If you feel your internal personal space line is being violated, all you can do is back up whenever he presses forward. Eventually he'll get the point. Later, when you have his confidence and trust and you're in a situation where you're sure you won't embarrass him, you can say something like "I know that in Brazil people come much closer to one another when they talk. We don't do that here. I wanted to tell you so that nobody misunderstands your actions."

If, on the other hand, you believe his closeness is sexual in nature, then you have every right to say firmly but kindly, "I would be much more comfortable if you would keep more of a distance." Remember not to accuse. Let the point go once you've made it. Be sensitive to the fact that, as an outsider, he will no doubt be embarrassed under even the best of circumstances.

Personality Conflicts

Q. ***My boyfriend drives me crazy. He never gives me a straight answer about anything. My mother says he's vague. How should I act with him?***

A. Sounds like you can drive him crazy by being your straightforward self and not wavering, so go for it. People who are consistently vague often are protecting their egos in one way or another. They generally won't let you know their motives because, if you knew, you might disagree and reject them or think less of them. Chances are your friend is drawn to you because he admires your directness. This may give you a great opportunity to learn how to accept another person for who he is without trying to make that person change to your way of thinking or acting. Your friendship might be a form of "agreeing to disagree." Just be yourself. Let him be himself. Recognize that you probably never will pin him down, so don't even try.

Public Displays of Affection

Q. ***My girlfriend always wants me to hold her hand when we're out. She's always kissing me when we go to games or the mall. I'm not used to it, and I'm embarrassed, but I don't want to hurt her. What should I do?***

A. All of us have different tolerance levels for public displays of affection. Your family may not show affection easily in front of others, for example, but your girlfriend's family may be extremely affectionate among themselves in public. The result is that you end up feeling uncomfortable with actions she considers very natural.

Much of how we view physical contact comes from our cultural heritage. Because the United States has so many cultures melting into one, it is important to be tolerant and not judge the behavior of others unfairly. For example, Asian cultures avoid all public physical contact. They don't even shake hands. Latin American and southern European cultures, on the other hand, are openly physical and affectionate, regardless of gender.

Be considerate of your girlfriend's feelings when you tell her how you feel. Remember that she probably will feel rejected and hurt. Do not point an accusing finger at her behavior; to do so could criticize her entire family and cultural heritage. Just be honest, sincere, and tell her gently how her physical behavior makes you feel. You can say something like "I'm embarrassed and uncomfortable when you always want to hold hands. I'm not really used to doing that around a lot of people. I like it when you hold my hand, and I like it when you kiss me, but not with an audience. Can we be a little more private?"

Be sure to tell her this at a time when you're alone and nobody can hear you. It would be very hurtful to her to sound like you're scolding her in public. Look her straight in the eye when you tell her so that she will understand that all you're asking for is a change in her physical behavior, not an end to the relationship.

From the tone of your letter, it seems that her behavior does not upset others around you the way more passionate behavior might. Hot and heavy action in public might feel good to people doing it but really embarrasses bystanders who have to watch it. That is rude behavior. All you have to do is think about how you would feel if you were with your little sister or your parents and happened upon two people in a passionate scene in the middle of the mall. Not a comfortable feeling, right?

We're usually the most defensive when we know we're wrong.

Punctuality

Q. ***My girlfriend is always late for everything. How can I tell her that this really makes me mad? I don't want to lose her, but it is driving me crazy.***

A. You have my sympathy. I'm pretty much a stickler for being on time. The single exception (I'm not proud to admit) used to be when I was doing something with my husband. I guess I thought that I could be more casual with him than with the rest of the world. This may be what is happening to you.

Of course the shoe was never on the other foot. He always was on time, probably just as you are. One day he just quietly said to me, "You know, five minutes mean a lot when I'm on my way to work." I got the message because he didn't sound angry when he told me and he used an example that was very important to him. That was the day I cleaned up my act.

You might try this approach. Don't get crazy and yell, sigh, look at your watch, pace the floor, or foam at the mouth. Those tactics just make the other person want to fight back in defense. Keep your cool and tell your girlfriend why it is important to you individually and to you as a couple to be on time. You might have to repeat this a time or two, but don't give up. Some people deal with chronic latecomers by lying about times and allowing an extra half hour. You can do that, but I don't believe in building relationships on lies, however small and innocent they seem. If the situation continues, instead of worrying about losing her you might stop calling and let her worry about losing you. I promise it will get her attention. Remind her that many people don't take seriously a person who is always late.

Hold the door for people behind you.

Standing for Others

Q. ***Why do men stand when women leave the room or table and stand again when they come back? I don't understand.***

A. Standing when a woman leaves or approaches is a tradition that makes her feel special, important, and protected. Many of our etiquette practices are based on behavior that was expected in the times of knights in armor. In those days a true gentleman openly displayed the qualities of chivalry—bravery, courtesy, and kindness. These qualities remain the mark of a gentleman today. Rising for a woman is a wonderful tradition that demonstrates you are living those qualities—and it still makes a woman feel special. In today's work arena, it is a courtesy that men extend to women—not mandatory behavior. Women should be secure and gracious enough to accept it.

Don't be shy about praising others if you really mean it.

Tact and Diplomacy

Q. ***My girlfriend won't talk to me. She got a new outfit, and when she asked me if I thought she looked fat in it, I said yes. What was I supposed to do?***

A. Oops. Bad move, dude. Whether or not your girlfriend is getting fat, questions regarding this delicate subject—like all questions about personal appearance—must be handled with tact and diplomacy. Most likely what she really is asking is "How do I look?" or "Do I please you?" If there isn't a serious weight-gain issue here (one that could indicate a health problem, for example) you could, and should, have come up with a more gentle response. You could have said something like "I really like the way you look in that outfit, but if you don't feel good in it, why don't you wear something else?"

You will learn that often people don't want honest answers to their questions. Sometimes they don't want an answer at all. And sometimes they just ask the wrong question. The ability to read between the lines and decipher what someone is really asking takes practice, patience, and a fair amount of understanding of the questioner. This is confusing, but I'll try to give you some guidelines.

I'm not a psychologist, but my experience tells me males are preoccupied with "how they perform" while females are preoccupied with "how they look." That's an oversimplification, but I've never yet met a guy who wanted a genuinely balanced critique to his question "What did you think of how I did in the football game?" And I know that if I ask my husband, "How do I look?" in an outfit I don't feel great about wearing, I'm actually asking him for reassurance and support that he likes what he sees.

Learning this will take time. Just keep your ears tuned for questions about personal appearance and remember what I've said.

Telephones

Q. ***When you're on the telephone with a boy, why would he not talk with you but instead talk to someone in his house? Why did he call you in the first place?***

A. His strange behavior may lead you to believe he's not all there, but he probably just doesn't know what he wants to say. Or, if he does know, he's afraid he'll sound dumb and you'll think less of him or laugh at him. Knowing this probably doesn't make you feel any better while you're hanging on the line waiting for him. It is silly to call somebody on the telephone and then not talk. In fact, in my book it is downright rude.

Tell your friend you would love to have a conversation with him, but since he called you, you shouldn't have to do all the talking. You can say something like "Listen, why are you calling me if you're not going to talk to me?" or "Why don't you finish talking with your brother and then call me back?"

Also remember that nobody feels very comfortable talking to a wall. Do your part to keep the conversation going. Ask him questions about what he did that day and be interested in, and listen to, his answers. Volunteer information about what you've been doing and what you're thinking about. Chances are that if you do your part to really engage him in conversation, he won't be so tongue-tied when he calls.

Unrequited Affection

Q. *How do you go about telling a person you don't like him or her when that person likes you and you don't want to hurt anyone's feelings?*

A. Obviously you've already realized that telling a person outright that you don't care for his or her company will result in badly hurt feelings. That's good. This is a situation that may occur throughout your life. The most important thing is to be extremely respectful and courteous whenever you're around this person. However, that does not mean you must accept invitations or go out of your way to engage in conversation. If you do receive an invitation from this person, say simply and kindly, "I'm sorry. I have other plans." Soon the message will become clear, and more than likely this person will steer clear of you. In the meantime, you will not have caused hurt, and neither of you will be embarrassed.

Q. ***A boy liked me for a while, so I called him a couple of times, but after a year I haven't called him since. I do like him, but right now I bet he doesn't like me anymore. What should I do?***

A. How much would you bet? There doesn't seem to be a lot you could lose by calling. You could gain by finding out the truth. In a situation like this there is nothing wrong with giving him a call. Keep in mind that a whole year has gone by since you talked with him. You might be thinking about calling him, but he may not have been thinking about you, so don't expect him to pick up where you left off. He'll probably feel awkward at first. Your job is to rekindle the friendship.

Say something like "Hi, Scott. This is Jen Martins. I haven't talked with you in so long, I've been wondering how you've been." Be sure to give your first and last name. Don't expect him to remember you out of context. It is easy to get tripped up and forget someone's name when you're surprised or don't expect to hear from him. That only makes for more embarrassment for both of you. He'll probably say hi and tell you he's fine. Guys in their teens aren't usually known for their conversation skills, so you'll have to nudge the conversation along by asking if he's still on the soccer team or getting along with his brother any better or something that you remember from your earlier relationship.

Judging by the way he responds, you can say something like "Some friends and I are getting together to see a movie Saturday. Would you like to join us?" The way he answers will give you a pretty good idea of how interested he is in seeing you again. And by the way you've asked the question, you haven't set yourself up for rejection or embarrassment because you haven't asked specifically for him to be your date. That approach is much kinder and considerate to both of you. Above all, don't push.

4
Relationships with Adults

"'After you,' is good manners. All doors open to courtesy."
Proverb

For parents . . .

This chapter may be difficult for you. It is about the guidelines of conduct that your children should use when relating to adults—including you.

It is important to understand that it is not about how you relate to your children . . . although you may learn much about how kids view you and other grown-ups.

Some of it may be painful, particularly the first section, devoted exclusively to etiquette with parents. The questions reflect youthful inexperience in dealing with life's most acute parental crises—fighting, divorce, unemployment. "Tell us how to act with our parents in the worst of times," these young people ask. If you've been in any of these situations, you may see your parenting skills reflected in the mistakes you've made or the clues you've missed. Don't take it personally. Parenting doesn't come with an instruction manual.

The rest of the chapter is devoted to relationships with other adults. As you might expect, these questions often challenge authority. For example, I receive very basic questions such as "Why do I have to respect adults?" and "Why can't I call adults by their first names?" These are difficult to answer unless you are prepared with the proper words and reasons.

When I began teaching etiquette to children, I felt like "Ms. Know-It-All" instead of Ms. Demeanor. That didn't last long. As they began asking questions, I realized they wanted to know the same things adults want to know. They just phrase it more bluntly. For example, an anxious child will ask, "When I go to Jane's birthday party, what if I don't know anybody? Who will I sit with? What should I talk about?" An adult will ask, "Do you give classes on how to work a room?"

That realization was humbling but valuable. After I caught on, I became much more successful at both teaching and writing for children. The key is fairly simple: realize that children possess basic, uncluttered wisdom. We cheat our children by failing to share our losses and insecurities, our joys and triumphs. We may do this in the mistaken belief that we are shielding them from life's harsh realities. It usually is a mistake. When you discover a commonality with your child, it is useful to say so with language like "I know. I feel the same way when. . . ." You will create a win-win situation and a receptive learning atmosphere.

Finally, beware of bullying. It is relatively easy to do inadvertently, simply because we're adults and bigger. Do I ever lose patience and bully? You bet. It is appropriate at times; when a child deliberately pushes you to see how far he or she can go, for example, it is fine to put your foot down. In general, however, try to empathize with your children—expressing your affinity empowers children and usually sparks their natural drive to learn more.

One final bit of advice: saying "when I was your age . . ." never works for me—unless I'm poking fun at myself.

Always remembver your parents' birthdays.

Relationships with Parents

Divorce

Q. ***My parents are getting a divorce. I haven't told anybody yet because I am so ashamed. What should I say?***

A. You've probably already heard this a million times, but your parents are not divorcing you; in fact their divorce has nothing to do with you. Their reasons—right or wrong—are their own. Still, it is a great and painful loss when parents divorce. I know. My parents divorced when I was a teenager. Don't make the mistake I did and not talk about it with friends.

If ever there was a time that you need support from friends, it is now. Be honest with them about how you feel—scared, angry, sad, cheated, abandoned, or the like. Good friends will listen, let you get things off your chest, and keep your conversation confidential if you ask them to. Talk with them quietly, outside from your busy schedule. That way you will be able to be honest about how you feel, and they can respond without being interrupted. Simply say "I have sad news. My parents are getting divorced." Trust that you will be fine and that you'll say the right thing.

There is no need to go into details by saying "Mom did this" or "Dad did that." Remain loyal to your parents. But there is nothing wrong with being honest about the way you feel. Let your friends nurture you a bit. You deserve and need it. And chances are you will someday find yourself in the position to do the same for somebody else.

Fighting

Q. ***If our parents are fighting, what should we do?***

A. It feels awful when our parents fight. We want to help or to stop it, but we really can't. We can stay out of their way, however. Never take sides. Fights between parents usually have nothing to do with you. Instead, go for a walk, visit a friend, play your Walkman with the earphones—just do something to isolate yourself from an argument that is painful for you.

Sooner or later things will calm down. Then you can talk with your parents and tell them how you feel when they argue. Perhaps you felt scared or angry or helpless. Tell them that—not who you think was right or wrong. If the fighting goes on a lot, you can look for outside opportunities to occupy your mind and time. For example, is there a club you would like to join? A part-time job you want? A volunteer project you could work on? These activities will balance the "down" feelings at home with good company and good times away.

Unemployment

Q. ***My dad lost his job last year. He used to make a lot of money, and I always had new clothes and things. Now I can't have new things until he gets another job, and I'm embarrassed at what my friends think. How should I act?***

A. There is nothing wrong with feeling bad about the situation you're in, so there is no point in pretending it doesn't hurt. The most important thing not to do is be embarrassed or ashamed, especially ashamed of your dad.

You are not alone even if it does feel that way right now. It takes a lot of courage to go through what your whole family is going through. When better times do come—and they will—you will be able to give yourself a pat on the back for maintaining dignity for yourself and your family.

Millions of American families are in the same position these days. The vast majority of them did not lose their jobs because of something they did or did not do. The economy is going through a very painful and complicated change. No true friend would tease you or make you feel less valuable because your family cannot afford to buy you new clothes. Doing your part to help your family put food on the table and keep a roof overhead should be far more important to you right now than dressing in style or being able to get that new CD that everybody at school is talking about. Besides, genuine dignity comes from what you have inside, not what you wear outside. Even the most luxurious clothes look shoddy on someone who doesn't feel good about herself.

You must avoid being (and looking) embarrassed. Make sure that everything you wear is clean and pressed, that your shoes are in good condition, and that you never leave the house without being carefully groomed—clean hair, face, and nails. You can update your wardrobe inexpensively by changing buttons, adding a new scarf or bangle bracelet, and making other small, inexpensive purchases here and there. Libraries have good selections of magazines filled with such tips on inexpensive chic. If you're old enough, you may want to get an after-school or weekend job to pay for your own new clothes—and don't forget to offer your parents some of what you earn to help with household expenses.

Finally, look at hard times as a learning experience. Do something. Let the situation motivate you to overcome it rather than being victimized by it and letting it depress or frighten you into inaction. I have never known a really successful person who has not gone through serious loss or difficulty sometime during his or her life.

Relationships with Other Adults

Conversation

Q. *What do I talk about when I meet my parents' friends for the first time?*

A. If you know that company is coming, ask your parents to tell you about the people ahead of time. Find out what they like to do, how they became friends, and whether they have their own children. That will make you more at ease when you meet them and give you hints on what to talk about. Strange as it sounds, talking with adults gets easier as you do it more. You can avoid dumb topics like how tall you are or how handsome you are by being the first to speak. Asking a good question is the best way to break a painful silence. "Do you live in our neighborhood?" works, for example. You also could ask about their children. I'm sure you will find that most adults like to talk about themselves and are glad to answer polite, sincere questions. Just be sure to pay attention and be interested in their answers.

Look people in the eye when speaking.

Q. *I never know what to talk about with my friend's parents. I feel really shy and stupid when I have to. What should I say?*

A. Being tongue-tied around people we don't know feels grim at any age. Solve this problem by remembering you and they have something in common: your friend, who is their child. Chances are your friend already has told them something abut you and experiences you've shared. So you always can start a conversation by saying something like "Jane and I are in the same history class. Did she tell you about our class project?"

If you are in their home, look around for conversation clues. You might see things like tennis racquets, roller blades, or skis and then know you can ask them if they do those sports. If you notice lots of plants or flowers, you might want to ask if gardening is a hobby for them.

Think back, too. Perhaps your friend has mentioned that his parents are baseball or basketball fans or like to read, for example. If so, you could ask if they went to a recent game or read a book that you've read. Try mentioning a movie you've seen and enjoyed or tell them about one you'd like to see and why you think it would be interesting.

Are there other children in the family besides your friend? You could ask about their hobbies or what schools they go to. Don't be afraid to give honest compliments. If you like the way their house looks or the brand of skis they own, say so.

The real trick to overcoming shyness in this situation is remembering that just about everybody is shy to a certain extent around new people or unfamiliar surroundings. The more you can stop worrying about yourself and focus on bringing out the people you're meeting, the better a conversationalist you'll become. Be a good listener, pay attention, and care about their answers. A valuable lesson to learn is that some people we all believe to be wonderful talkers actually say very little—but they listen a lot to what we say.

When all else fails, use a system invented by Eleanor Roosevelt. She used the alphabet as a subject file and would think of things that began with the letter *A*—like apples, art, ancestors, accidents, and so on—and pick one she guessed would most likely interest her new companion. If nothing starting with the letter *A* sparked a conversation, she went on to things beginning with *B* and so on. In her book, *Eleanor Roosevelt's Book of Common Sense Etiquette* she writes that very few people required going beyond *C*.

First Names

Q. ***Why can't I call adults by their first names?***

A. You can if they invite you to do so. It is just plain rude (even for adults) to call other adults by their first names when they don't know you or you them. Unfortunately, this happens all the time and the rules are changing because of it. It is impolite to assume the privileges of a familiar relationship before you have one. When you meet an adult, call him or her Mr., Mrs., or Ms. (pronounced "Mizz") until he or she asks you to use a first name. It is up to the adult to make that decision. Sometimes it happens quickly. Sometimes it takes a while. And sometimes it never happens.

Never call adults by their first names unless they give you permission.

Foreign Languages

Q. ***Can I speak in my ethnic language when there is an adult guest in our house who doesn't understand it?***

A. Of course you can, but guests always should be included in the conversation so they don't feel left out or, worse, talked about behind their backs. Just about everybody is more comfortable talking in their native language, but it should always be translated as best you can for guests so that they feel truly welcome and part of the conversation. You've probably been in this situation, so you know how important it is to reassure your guests that you're not talking about them when they cannot understand.

My father's family was from another country. They spoke another language that I did not understand. They never helped me learn it, and they never took the time to put me at ease when they spoke it. The result was that I avoided going to their homes because I always felt left out. Be sure you don't make your visitors feel that way.

Friends of Parents

Q. ***Why do I have to be nice to my father's friend?***

A. Technically speaking, you don't have to be nice to anyone. You can choose whether you treat people with consideration and respect, or with contempt. As a human being you have free will. I am sure you know many examples of people who use that free will to choose to treat others with contempt. At one extreme they are muggers, murderers, and other criminals. At the other extreme they are just those unpleasant, negative people you don't like to be around. I can give you more direction on how to get along with people better and make your life more harmonious, but I never would tell you that you have to do something. That would be an insult to your intelligence and free will.

In answer to your question, since your father deserves respect not only because he's your father but also because he is a fellow human being, it follows logically that his friends deserve the same respect and courtesy. That does not mean that you have to like your father's friend or that you have to make that person your own friend. It simply means that you should make every effort to be considerate, not rude.

Say hello and shake hands. Offer this person refreshments when appropriate. Acknowledge this person's presence when you're in the same room by making conversation and listening politely. Think about how you would feel if the shoe were on the other foot. What kind of consideration would you expect, for example, from the father of one of your friends who might not like you? Would you expect him to roll his eyes or give you icy stares or throw a temper tantrum if you and he were in the same room?

Have you told your father about how you feel around his friend? It is not up to you to choose his friends, but it is fair to tell him calmly how you feel about this person. Do not speak in anger or make accusations. Above all, do not attack your father. You may not understand the full details of his relationship with his friend.

Gifts

Q. ***What should I say when a relative gives me a gift that I think is silly or ugly and I don't like it?***

A. I bet you've heard the expression, "It's the thought that counts." It is important to accept graciously any gift you're given. Gift giving highlights the fact that not everybody shares the same tastes. If they did, what a boring world this would be.

When you open a gift that makes you want to cry or laugh out loud, be diplomatic instead. Say "Thank you. It was really nice of you to think of me." After all, it truly is the thought that counts, and the giver thinks enough of you to take the trouble to make or purchase a gift. If the giver presses you further and asks outright if you like it, simply say "Of course I like it. You gave it to me."

You won't please anybody
if you try to please everybody.

Greetings

Q. ***My grandmother always makes me shake hands with new people who come to our house. Do I have to?***

A. You sure do. She is teaching you a really good habit. Don't do it just because she is around. If someone offers his or her hand to shake, you are being offered a gesture of friendship. Shake hands with a firm grip, a smile, and look the person straight in the eye. Say "Hello Mrs. Nash" or "How do you do?" Remember that the first thing you should do when you are introduced to anyone is to stand up and offer your hand.

Q. ***When you are in a room and another person walks in, who is supposed to speak first? Many people have told me it depends on age. Is this true?***

A. Many of us were taught as children not to speak to adults unless they speak to us first. That isn't necessarily the case today. If you enter a room, you should greet the person who is there. It doesn't matter whether you are younger or older. If you are in a room and someone enters, go ahead and greet that person. The person who makes eye contact first should start the conversation. Think of how unfriendly you would appear if you waited to be spoken to first. The most important thing about good manners is to put those around you at ease. If that means speaking first, look the person in the eye, smile, and speak.

Kissing

Q. ***What do you do when your aunt wants to kiss you and you don't want to?***

A. Sometimes we just have to put up with discomfort. Unwanted affection is common, and not just in the family. Even adults in the business world experience it. You could try extending your hand to shake before she gets close. You'll have to practice this technique. It isn't easy. Once you are in her clutches, however, diversionary tactics are tougher to execute. Try turning your head slightly so that you end up with a light brush on the cheek. That won't hurt her feelings since you haven't exactly rejected her kiss. And if she has any brains at all, she'll get the message that you are not crazy about kissing. If she doesn't get the message, the next time (before you're in the clutch) say something like, "I'm not much of a kisser. Let's shake hands instead."

Mom's Boyfriend

Q. ***My mother's new boyfriend is always buying me gifts and trying to be extra-nice to me. I like him OK, but I would like him better if he would stop giving me gifts so that he can get in good with Mom. What should I do?***

A. Tell your mother that the gifts make you feel uncomfortable. She will pass the message to her boyfriend quickly enough. If you must tell him yourself, state your feelings simply and honestly without accusing him of anything as you did in your question. Thank him for all he has done for you, but tell him that you would rather not receive gifts from him because it makes you feel like he's just using them to try to please your mother. Chances are good that he will stop and think about how he would feel in your shoes. If you end up being friends, both of you will have the best gift of all.

Respect

Q. ***Why do I have to respect older people?***

A. Wouldn't it be nice if everyone you met treated you with courtesy and kindness, helped you when you needed it, and accepted you for no reason other than just who you are? If that happened, everyone you met would be treating you with respect. It is the way all people should treat other people, especially older people, who have seen, heard, and experienced so much of life. Of course, to get treated this way we must do the same to others. After all, it has to start somewhere. Imagine how this world would be if everybody treated everybody else with respect and kindness. Wouldn't it be a much nicer place? Each of us can play a part in making it happen by treating others as we would like to be treated. Old advice, but I'm glad you asked. It always deserves repeating.

Don't make your neighbors crazy by playing your stereo loudly.

Salespeople

Q. ***When I go shopping, the salesperson always takes care of me last, even if I was first, if adults are there. Is it rude to say something?***

A. Nobody likes to be ignored. If you're in a store waiting for service and the salesperson intentionally ignores you, you have every right to speak up. Sometimes adults do kids a disservice by not taking them seriously. Adults can be guilty of that not only in stores but also at school and on the telephone. The most important part of speaking up is how you do it. You have to walk the diplomatic tightrope by being firm but respectful at the same time. We actually train people around us how to treat us by the way we treat them.

Remember the way you like to be treated before you let off steam. Simply say to the salesperson, "Excuse me, I think I'm next in line. I'd like to see the green sweatshirt, please." If the salesperson seems to be ignoring you when there are no other customers around, just say, "Could you please help me?" If you find you are ignored frequently at the same store, shop elsewhere and let the manager know you intend to do so in a polite note. If you are a courteous shopper, you deserve better treatment.

Thank the cash register clerk when you buy something.

Smoking

Q. ***Is it OK to ask an adult to stop smoking? I really hate smoke.***

A. Of course you can, but it depends on where you are. I wouldn't ask people to stop smoking in their own homes or elsewhere in private where smoking is permitted and perhaps encouraged by the presence of ashtrays and other go-ahead signals.

However, in public places—particularly those where smoking is prohibited—go ahead and ask, but do it correctly. Smoke is a proven health hazard of widespread significance. It is potentially fatal to the smoker and may present a problem, called *secondary smoke* to those nonsmokers nearby. A polite "Would you please stop smoking or smoke somewhere else?" is all you really have to say. The skill is in learning to say it in a manner that does not condemn the smoker and simply sounds matter-of-fact.

To practice this tone, try standing in front of a mirror and repeating "It's raining outside." Then, in the same tone of voice, without emotion, try saying "Would you please stop smoking?"

I urge you to practice before doing it in real situations. Making a person feel guilty about smoking, especially a stranger, is just as rude as blowing smoke in someone's face. Fortunately, most new working environments and schools are now smoke-free by law. However, there still are many public places where smoking is allowed. Therefore, people do have the right to smoke. In cases like this, a smoker quite legitimately can refuse your request.

Offer advice only when you're asked for it.

Work

Q. ***I'm not old enough to get a job in a real company, but I want to earn money over the summer. I can do odd jobs and help people. What's the best way to do this? I'm honest and dependable.***

A. I wish you lived in my neighborhood. I can think of a dozen jobs I'd like help with. I'm sure your neighbors could, too. You probably will be busier than you ever would expect if you put the word out. That's why it is particularly important to get organized from the beginning.

First, decide what types of jobs you are willing to do. Be sure you do these things really well. You don't want any unsatisfied customers. Bad news travels quickly. For example, some things most people would welcome having done well around the house include small painting jobs (fences, doors, and so forth), washing and waxing cars, fixing bikes and toys, watching and walking pets, baby-sitting and child care (including keeping children safe and occupied when moms are at home but busy with other chores or running short errands), and doing laundry and ironing.

There also are traditional jobs like delivering newspapers or mowing lawns. These are just some ideas to get you thinking. I'm sure you can discover many more on your own.

When you leave telephone messages, be sure to include your number.

After you have decided what services you can offer, determine the rates you will charge. The simplest ways are either per hour or per job. If you select the per-hour method, customers will want to know how long you expect each job to take. Be sure to have some estimates in your head and assure them that if you cannot get the job done in the time you estimated, you will speak with them for permission before working extra time and charging them for it. For example, it might take you four hours to paint a garage door, but it might take six hours if the old paint needs scraping and sanding before you can start. Be prepared with those facts. It looks unprofessional to hesitate when a potential customer asks how long a job will take. When you are sure enough of yourself to estimate correctly, you build customer confidence.

The next step is to advertise. Put together a flier or postcard with your name, telephone number, and a list of services. Make sure your flier has no spelling or punctuation mistakes and is easy to read. Make it look crisp and clean. Black type on bright yellow paper is an eye-catching combination. Get your message directly into the hands of neighbors by going from door to door. Post your flier on a community bulletin board. Get it into the hands of local merchants who might want to hire you to help in their stores or businesses. Do this in person. Be sure to look well groomed. Keep your nails and hair clean. Wear decent clothes. If you are calling on business owners, it wouldn't hurt to make sure you're wearing a nice pair of slacks instead of jeans and sneakers. Remember, you're asking people to trust you by hiring you. People will notice the difference. Remain well-groomed after you're hired. Nobody likes to deal with a slob.

When you call on prospective customers, ask for a convenient time. Don't try to schedule appointments during the dinner hour or at the peak customer time for a store. In a store, ask for the owner or manager. In private homes, see the person responsible for running the house. There is no need to go inside a private home. You can accomplish your mission at the front door. When you are face-to-face with the person you came to see, introduce yourself, smile, maintain eye contact, and don't fidget or chew gum. Practice this with your parents. You'll feel a bit silly at first, but it is important that you learn how to state your case clearly in a minute or two. That's about all the time you'll get to sell yourself.

If someone hires you to do a job, set a time, thank the person, and leave. If the person you're speaking with is hesitant about hiring you, leave your flier and ask if you can come back in two days.

Do your best to return phone calls within twenty-four hours.

Be sure to get a Social Security number if you don't have one. You can apply for your Social Security number at the post office. Keep good records of what you earn.

Most important, always remember that the true test of success in business is whether your customers refer you to more new customers and call you back themselves for other work. This will depend on how well you do the job, how honest you are, and how well you keep your word. Never lie to cover up a mistake. Never make false claims to build yourself up. Customers will find out eventually.

5
Relationships with Peers

"Keep your friendships in repair."
Ralph Waldo Emerson

To parents . . .

By all standards, children ask more questions about their relationships with other children than any other topic. I believe this is a good omen. It proves that Mother Nature instills a tendency to be kind. With a little nurturing—and perhaps this instruction manual—that tendency can be developed into a habit that will last a lifetime.

Children assume they should be naturally liked and accepted no matter how they act. But friendships, like all relationships, require balance and patience. We need multiple friends because we have multiple interests. That variety of interests causes us to invite many different people into our lives. For example, in my own life I have a friend who loves to run as much as I do, so we're running buddies. I treasure our exercise times together. Another friend is a movie buff like me, but her idea of exercise is turning the pages of a book. I am as close to her as a sister. The three of us are friends, but we seek each other out for different yet equally important reasons. It is from this very normal dichotomy that conflict in peer relationships arises.

When something goes wrong with your child's relationship with a classmate or friend, there are things you can teach that will help define and approve the value of differences between people. Rather than learning rejection, your child can find—and extend—acceptance. You can teach that the way to be a good friend is to be the best person possible, to cultivate and share his or her own interests and to encourage friends to do the same. That way time spent with friends is much more interesting. There is more to talk about. Friendships last longer and stay fresher. Friendships become stronger because they support each other rather than becoming one-sided or controlling.

By example you also can teach your child the importance of letting friends know how special they are. Your refusal to take your relationship with your own child for granted will demonstrate that they, in turn, should not assume their own friendships will last forever without some effort. Friendships denied nurturing usually die of neglect.

By example, you also can teach that friends should be encouraged to find the space and support they need to explore individual activities and new people. Those friends, in turn, should be willing to share new experiences and not feel obligated to apologize for striking out on their own. When we feel supported and encouraged by another human being, we naturally return to the source of that support.

Finally, when rejection by or directed at peers does threaten to invade your child's life, you can suggest standing in that friend's shoes for a moment. Encourage your child to examine personal behavior with another's eyes and ears. Your child may discover something new and different about himself and the nature of friendships: when friends are treated with kindness and dignity—the way all of us wish to be treated—the payoff is the ability to be and have real friends.

Borrowing and Lending

Q. ***I lent my friend five dollars from my allowance. He never paid me back. What should I do?***

A. This breach of trust is unfortunate, but it happens every day, even in business or between adult friends. There is a polite way to handle this unpleasant situation, however. First, give your friend the benefit of a doubt. He may have forgotten about your loan. You can say "Hey, did you forget about my five dollars? I could use it."

If it looks like he's trying to squirm out of it, ask him politely but firmly for the money. Say something like "Didn't you agree to pay back that five dollars you borrowed? When are you going to do that? It's important." If he cannot return the loan all at once, agree to let him pay you a dollar a week or according to other terms. Be clear about which day the money is due, or you might end up back at square one. If he refuses to keep his agreement, you then must decide whether to ask for help from an adult. This is much the way it's done in the business world.

Q. ***Is it bad manners to borrow money from a friend?***

A. No, but it is bad manners and bad business to borrow and not repay. Respect an agreement to pay back a friend just as you would if you had borrowed from a bank. Be clear about exactly when and how you will repay. Write a letter in ink that confirms the agreement. It doesn't have to be stuffy and formal. Just say something like "Dear Danny: Thank you for lending me ten dollars today. I will pay you back five dollars a week for the next two weeks. I plan to give you the money on Tuesdays." Date and sign the letter. Doing this prevents any misunderstandings and keeps your friendship intact.

Cheating

Q. ***I wrote a poem and submitted it to my school anthology. Then my friend read my poem, copied it, and changed a couple of lines. My friend also submitted it to the anthology and made my library teacher think she wrote it. Now it looks like I'm a copycat. I tried to talk to my friend, but she wouldn't listen. I don't trust her anymore, but I still am kind of friendly with her. How should I approach my friend to tell her how rude she was?***

A. Have you ever noticed that we least want to hear the truth when we know, in our hearts, we're wrong? I know that I am most defensive when I'm wrong. I don't want mistakes thrown back in my face. You said your friend wouldn't listen to you. On the contrary, I suspect she heard you very well and, down deep, she's ashamed of claiming your poem as hers.

You are dealing with two major disappointments here: not receiving full credit for your work and a friend's disloyalty and dishonesty. There's an old saying: "You can't cheat an honest man." It means when something is ours alone, it can never truly be taken from us. In this case you're learning a valuable lesson early in life. The reality is that you must take whatever precautions necessary to protect your work. I bet you'll never again show your work to anyone before you submit it to your school anthology. As you get older, you'll remember this as you write term papers, theses, and maybe even your first book. For now, knowing that the poem is yours is what really matters. You should tell your teacher in private what happened so that she has a chance to understand.

Beyond that, talking about it and complaining about your friend will only cause you to lose self-respect and the respect of your peers. You can always create more and better poems, but your reputation can't be re-created.

Betrayal by a friend is very painful. Before you lose your cool and become self-righteous, try to see things from her viewpoint. If she honestly felt as talented as you, she would have written her own poem rather than copying yours. I'll bet that, even though she appears to ignore what you say, she feels really bad about what she did.

If I were you, I would tell her how I felt but bite my tongue if I felt like beating her up verbally. You can say something like "Look, I'm really hurt that you took my poem. It hurts most because I showed it to you because I trusted you and wanted to know what you thought of it. I feel you betrayed me. I can't trust you anymore, and that hurts because I care a lot about you as my friend." No matter how gentle you are, she probably will feel attacked, so after you've said it, leave it alone. For the moment, you will have done all you can. She will feel awkward around you for a while. Unless she has done other things like this before, you should continue being friendly. A true friendship should not be discarded because of a single transgression.

Death in the Family

Q. ***I am having a party soon. I want to invite my friend, but her brother died a week ago. Is it OK to invite her?***

A. I applaud your sensitivity. Your friend may not feel much like partying, but I think it would hurt her to feel excluded. After all, this is a time when she needs friends more than ever. Despite your good intentions, if you were to ignore her and say nothing, you probably would confuse her and make her think something is wrong with her because her brother died.

Give her a choice on whether to attend. No doubt she will

be guided by her family's views and religious beliefs. Say something like "I'm having a party and would love you to be there. I know it hasn't been very long since your brother died, so I know you might not feel like partying, but I just want you to know how welcome you are."

Just listening is one of the best gifts you can give a friend.

Q. ***What do you say to a friend when her father has died?***

A. The simplest words are the best. Look your friend in the eye and say "I'm so sorry." Don't forget to ask how she's doing. Then listen carefully and let her tell you. She might cry, but that's OK; she needs to. Rambling on really won't help. If you want, you can recall an anecdote involving her father that was particularly meaningful to you, perhaps a hike you all took together or a game you attended. Bringing the deceased person's life into focus helps create warm feelings for the family. The most important thing to remember about offering your condolences is not words but actions. Be there for your friend in the days after the funeral, when she'll feel the loss more acutely than ever. Even if you don't say anything at all, she will appreciate having someone there who cares.

Q. ***My grandfather died three years ago, but friends still ask me how he is doing. What would be a polite way to tell them he died without making them feel like they hurt my feelings?***

A. Congratulations on your insight. You realize you could embarrass someone who innocently asks about your grandfather, unaware that he has died. The very essence of good manners is to be concerned and sensitive about the feelings of others.

The answer to your question is easier than you might expect. All you have to say is "Thank you for asking. Unfortunately, he died a while ago. We miss him a lot, and he would be pleased to know that you asked about him." Avoid going into a long story about his death. Instead, gently change the subject. It would be a good time to say you're glad to see the person and to ask about how he or she is. Ask about family, school, or job. Pay attention and be interested in the answers. You'll quickly move from discomfort to ease.

Fighting

Q. ***I just had a fight with my best friend. What can we do to solve the problem and be friends again?***

A. All strong, lasting friendships endure their share of rocky times. It's just logical. Everyone is different. There is bound to be conflict. Don't be too discouraged. Sometimes the conflict that first upset you can bring you closer together. How you handle it will make the difference.

The most important thing to remember is to handle your conflict directly, person to person. I know it often feels easier and safer to be indirect or to ignore the situation by giving each other the cold shoulder, to say hurtful things, or to gossip. However, these actions will never mend a friendship. If you've fought, chances are good that both of you said things in anger that you didn't mean. What you must do first is be honest with yourself. You must have a clear understanding of exactly what you said or did and why.

When you are sure of these details, it is time to speak to your friend alone. Tell your friend that you're feeling bad because you did or said such-and-such. Say exactly how you feel. Say you are upset because of how important the friendship is to you. Say you would like to repair any damage done during the fight. If an apology is in order, by all means apologize simply and from the heart. Don't rehash the fight. Don't attack your friend again.

Differences between people are healthy. You don't have to roll over to your friend's side of the argument to regain the friendship. You would lose your self-respect if you did that, and in the end your friend would lose respect for you. The best you can do is acknowledge your friend's right to his or her own opinions and be responsible for your position and feelings. You can't change your friend, but you can be open to new ideas and beliefs and let your friend know how much better and happier your life is because of it.

Disagreements don't ruin friendships; disrespect does.

Q. ***Two of my friends are in a fight. They want me to take sides. What should I do?***

A. Let both friends know how important they are to you, but don't take sides and don't talk about either friend. It is appropriate to say something like "I can understand why you're so upset." It is fair to let each side know that the other is upset. It might help them resolve the issue. Just remember that they must make up their own minds and settle this themselves. A fight between friends is one case where advice is often asked but rarely really wanted.

Q. ***I said something really mean and hurt my friend's feelings. I just wasn't thinking. Now I feel awful. What should I do?***

A. Don't let the grass grow under your feet. Apologize now. You don't have to rehash everything you said. Hearing it will only hurt again. Just be honest and sincere. Tell your friend you were inconsiderate and thoughtless. Apologize. Say that you would never deliberately say or do anything to be mean or spiteful—and then hope you're forgiven. Don't beat yourself up over this. We all do thoughtless things without considering what happens later. Learn from this unfortunate incident.

Learning to apologize is one of life's most useful skills.

Fitting In

Q. ***I'm new in the neighborhood, and I've been invited to a party. I don't know what to wear to fit in. What should I do?***

A. When in doubt, ask. Your invitation should have included that information. Since that wasn't the case, call your host or hostess. Tell him or her that you're not sure what to wear. Most likely, you'll be told what he or she is planning to wear—

maybe jeans and a T-shirt or a skirt and blazer—and that will guide you.

Don't try to change your friends. Enjoy them for the special people they are.

Q. ***All my friends are getting their own telephones and televisions for their rooms. My parents won't let me. What can I tell my friends? I'm embarrassed at how mean they are.***

A. Life is so much easier when our parents and friends agree with the way we think, isn't it? Your parents are giving you a super opportunity to learn to respect and accept the values of others. As time goes by, we learn that part of getting along in life requires honoring the positions of others—even when we don't agree, even when those values and positions make us uncomfortable or angry.

If your friends ask why you don't have your own television or telephone, tell them that your parents believe one telephone or television is enough. You don't have to pretend that their decision makes you happy or that you understand it. That's just the way it is.

Remember also that multiple appliances are a drain on the Earth's resources. Using only what you need is the mark of true sophistication and savvy when it comes to being a responsible citizen of this planet. If you see the wisdom in this, try telling your friends. Be careful not to sound spiteful or superior. When you have a good reason behind what you say, you don't have to say it in a nasty way. Good reasons, well stated, give others something to think about.

Q. ***What should I do when I'm with a group of people and I don't understand what they're talking about?***

A. I wish I had a nickel for every time this has happened to me. First, don't feel dumb. We all prefer to, or feel we should, participate in conversations. We should try, but it isn't always possible to be an active participant, especially if we're clueless about the topic.

However, it is always possible to be an active listener. This is the polite way to go. Don't sigh, moan, roll your eyes, or yawn when you're in the dark. Don't be embarrassed or ashamed about not understanding. Nobody can be an expert on everything. If someone asks your opinion and you don't have one because you don't know enough, say that. As long as you're paying attention and asking brief questions when you are confused, you're fine.

On the flip side, use your experience to be sure you are never the one to be carrying on a long conversation that leaves someone else out. That is very rude. Always draw out the quiet ones in any conversation so they feel welcome and at ease.

Invitations and Visits

Q. ***A friend called and asked if I could come to her house. I said yes, and then another friend called a few minutes later and asked the same thing. What do I do?***

A. If you accepted the first invitation, it is important to keep your agreement. Go and have a good time. Tell the second friend that you've already made plans. You don't have to explain where you're going. Just be sure to be sensitive to your friend's feelings. Nobody likes to be told no. It would be a good idea to suggest another plan. You can say something like "I have other plans for Saturday. What about Sunday? I'd love to visit you then."

Q. ***If my friends ask me to go to the mall, and I don't feel like going, what should I say?***

A. It is a compliment that your friends invite you to join them. It means they like your company and have fun with you. It is correct and understandable that you don't especially want to hurt their feelings by saying no, but it is certainly OK to say "Sorry, I don't feel like going to the mall today, but thanks for asking. I'll go next time." However, remember that friendships require give-and-take. If you turn down their invitations too many times, they'll stop asking. Sometimes it is better to go even when you don't especially want to. Working at maintaining those friendships is more important than the specific activity.

Learn from your friends. You should be interested in what they're doing.

Q. ***I've been invited to my friends' house in Florida for a week at spring break. How should I act?***

A. Remember that your friends invited you because they enjoy your company and want more of it, so above all be yourself. The most important thing about being a houseguest is remembering to be pleasant and courteous to everyone in the household, not just the person who invited you. Be sure to go along with the family's routine even if you're used to having meals at different times or they love to play volleyball and you don't. Take part in their activities and be a good sport about it.

We all need quiet time alone. Be prepared to respect your host family's need for this. Take along a book or deck of cards to entertain yourself during those times. Keep your room neat and clean. Be sure to keep yourself neat and clean, too. Leave the bathroom more orderly than you find it. Take your friend's parents a gift such as chocolates or fancy nuts and give it to them when you arrive.

Send a thank-you note as soon as you get home and explain what a good time you had. Mention the highlights of your visit. For example, if it was the first time you tried water-skiing and enjoyed it, say so. If you keep these things in mind and actually do them, everybody will be glad you were a houseguest and will be eager to have you back.

Q. ***My friend always messes up my room when she comes over, so my mom said she couldn't come over anymore. I don't know how to tell her. What should I say?***

A. If you've never spoken to your friend about the mess she makes, it's worth asking your mom for one more chance. If she says yes, don't rush to invite your messy friend back. Let some time go by. When she mentions another trip to your house, tell her that house rules are tighter than the last time she visited and that you're expected to clean up after yourselves. Tell her the rules apply to everyone, including guests. Add that if she wants to come over she has to do her share and help you. If she isn't willing to do that, suggest that you go to her house instead. When you're her guest, be careful to clean up after yourself. The best way to persuade people to do something is to set a good example.

Q. ***If you're invited to a birthday party and can't go, should you send a gift anyway?***

A. It depends on how close you are to the person being honored. You don't absolutely have to send a gift, but if you want to, you really should. It is a great way to let your friend know how much you care and that you would have been there if possible.

Q. ***We always visit my cousins at Christmas. One of them was born on New Year's Eve, but we never give him a birthday gift because his birthday is so close to Christmas and we give Christmas gifts. I think we should give him something for his birthday, too. Do you?***

A. In twenty years your cousin probably will be thankful that his birthday gets lost in the holiday hubbub. Now, however, chances are good he feels ripped off; it probably feels as if he doesn't have the birthday celebration that everybody else has. There is one benefit: he'll never have to go to school on his birthday.

I applaud you for being sensitive to his feelings. If you give your other cousins birthday gifts, it is only fair to give him one, too. If you don't give birthday presents to the others, there is no reason to give him one just because you're there at Christmas. That wouldn't be fair to your other cousins. You could, however, make sure his birthday is special by doing some very simple and easy things. Give him a birthday card—one that isn't a Christmas card with "Happy Birthday" scribbled at the bottom. Make it yourself if you can. This will let him know that his special day wasn't forgotten during the rush of the holiday season.

A final suggestion: continue to remember his birthday as you get older. He will really appreciate it and treasure you for that.

Q. ***What's the proper way to answer a telephone when you're at a friend's house?***

A. It is rude to answer someone else's phone without permission. If, however, nobody from the household is nearby, it is a real kindness simply to pick up the phone and say, "Hello, Smith residence." In that way callers will at least know that hearing an unfamiliar voice does not mean they got the wrong number.

Q. ***We have a pool in our backyard. It is the only one in the neighborhood. All my friends keep telling me they can't wait to hang out this summer. That's going to make my mom really mad. Besides, the kids who say that aren't all my good friends. What should I do?***

A. It is not surprising that you might find yourself drowning in fair-weather friends this summer. And you're probably correct in thinking that they're more interested in a cool dip in your pool than your friendship. Don't take it too personally. It is human nature. You'll learn that sort of thing happens over and over.

On the other hand, you probably don't want to be the only fish in your personal pond all the time. Why not craft a compromise that would be acceptable to all, including your mom? Before a group swoops down on you, bathing suits in hand, talk with your mom and ask if she would mind if your friends visit occasionally. If she says yes, you can establish specific visiting days and times—perhaps something like every other Friday afternoon from two to five. That way you've already established your policy. When the question comes up, you can say "My parents said I can have guests at the pool on Friday afternoons from two to five. If you want to come then, it would be great." You've set the boundaries and been gracious and fair.

Remember to tell your friends they're responsible for their own towels and refreshments—and for cleaning up afterward—if that's the case.

Q. ***What do you do when your sneakers are wet and muddy and you go to a friend's house? Is it OK to take them off?***

A. If your feet are soaking wet and you're going to make a mess of the house, tell your friend you have to remove them and ask to borrow a fresh pair of socks. Wear the borrowed socks home. Be sure to return them as soon as they are laundered. I know you might feel silly at someone else's house in socks, but it's fine in this case because it makes sense and you were kind enough not to get the floor wet or muddy. By the way, in the Japanese culture it is considered impolite to wear shoes indoors. Removing one's shoes is a way of demonstrating respect in that country.

Classy kids are gracious when they lose.

Q. ***If one of my best friends is having a party and doesn't invite me, what should I do?***

A. First, are you sure that you haven't been invited? Sometimes best friends just assume that the people closest to them will be there without an official invitation. That's not right, but it happens.

You have an opportunity to learn and teach here. It is likely that sometime before the party other friends will ask you if you plan to go. Answer directly and honestly. Say "I don't plan to go because I haven't been invited." Say it without sounding angry or accusatory. The truth is that it is the host's right to invite the people he wants to the party. In your position it is tough to figure out why you are excluded, but you must respect the choice. I know how disappointing your situation can be. You'll have to smile through it and be kind and gracious.

If you don't end up going, don't ask the people who did attend a lot of questions about it. That will only make them feel uncomfortable. Remember that not being invited to a party does not mean nobody likes you. It also doesn't mean you're a bad person or something is wrong with you. Being excluded from your friend's party might have been caused by something as simple as the fact that you're at her house all the time but she has not been that generous with other friends and it is time to share a bit more with the others. If you act with kindness toward her and everybody else and don't make anybody feel bad, you can show how classy you are.

Meeting and Parting

Q. ***Why do I have to say hello back when friends say hello, and why do I have to greet people who come to my house?***

A. A greeting is the first thing that happens between two people. It forms the basis of our relationship with another person. As a movie or book has a beginning and end, so must a conversation. Think about seeing a movie at the theater. You are all set to enjoy it, but you can't follow the plot because the movie has no beginning or end. You become confused, and when you leave the theater you think either that it was a bad movie because it didn't make any sense or that you missed

---

Remember to smile.
You'll usually get one back.

---

something important. It's the same thing for greetings and farewells.

Everything in life has a beginning and an end. For common greetings between friends (or anybody, for that matter) always say hello and good-bye. Saying hello starts conversations and gets people to talk. Saying good-bye makes people feel good about where they've been and makes them want to return. Saying hello and good-bye also gives us a chance to make new friends.

Q. ***How do I tell my best friend that I'm moving?***

A. Your friend is fortunate that you think enough of her to be concerned about her feelings. Moving is tough for anybody. Most people get so caught up in the move themselves that they ignore its impact on everybody else.

The best way to handle this situation is honestly and simply. As with all difficult emotional events, the language should be plain and kind. The challenge is actually to get the words out when you know you could be about to hurt someone. You might want to say something like this: "I'm moving. I'm going to miss you very much. Let's spend time together before I move and figure out how we can see each other afterward." Be sure to tell your friend how much she means to you so she won't feel abandoned. If you really are her best friend, you'll stay in touch by letter or telephone if it can't be face-to-face.

Personal Habits

Q. ***I have a friend that I have lunch with sometimes. He blows his nose with a honking sound, and it makes me sick. What should I do?***

A. Ahhh, your chicken salad is delicious, and you're having a great conversation in the cheerful, crowded lunchroom, when all of a sudden your dining partner whips out a handkerchief the size of a tablecloth and blows his nose loudly. So loudly, in fact, that the entire room becomes silent for fifteen seconds. The offender is oblivious to his disturbance, crumbles the mess into a ball, and stuffs the wad back into his pocket. Sound familiar?

Handling your friend's honking habit is easier said than done. Here's one way: These moments of truth between friends often are tense and sensitive. Humor helps—if you can avoid being sarcastic. The next time the honking happens, look your friend in the eye and say something like "You know, I really value our friendship, so I have to tell you how much that disturbs me and that I think it can be embarrassing to you even if you don't know it." Although the initial reaction may be denial and anger, a true friend will see your point and change the habit.

Above all, proceed gently. Don't attack as you might be tempted to do when you feel uncomfortable and anxious. Any distraction that affects our senses adversely during mealtime is offensive and therefore bad manners. When we ignore these basic rules, we find ourselves dining alone most of the time. Some of the most common infractions (besides nose blowing) are cracking gum, chewing food loudly with an open mouth, or not being well groomed. Unwashed hair, dirty clothes, or grimy fingernails don't exactly spark an appetite.

Q. ***My friend is always making loud noises and talking in the movie theater. I like her, but I can never understand the movie. What should I do?***

A. Unfortunately, kids aren't the only people who interrupt movies and shows with talking and noises. Adults do it, too. Tell your friend that you can't understand the film because of her noises. Ask her to stop. If she is loud the next time, find a new movie pal and save your rowdy friend for ball games, where shouting is part of the program. Be sure that you don't deliberately embarrass her in front of others. There are many other ways in which people are inconsiderate at the movies. Be sure you're not kicking the chair in front of you, putting your feet up on it, or making lots of trips to the snack bar after the movie has started.

Q. ***How do you tell your friend he has bad breath without hurting his feelings?***

A. Your question boils down to something we all face sooner or later: how do you tell someone you care for that there is something unpleasant about him or her? The expression "What are friends for?" applies here. Friends are for support. When you support someone, you do it all the time, not just when you're having fun. Real support means you have the duty to point out to your friend that something is wrong, even though it may be embarrassing. It would be more embarrassing to let the situation continue. That's not something you should be willing to let happen if you have the power to stop it.

Be prepared for anger at first, but in the long run a real friend will understand you are helping to prevent future embarrassment. How to break the news is rather simple. Always do it when you are alone and nobody else is within hearing distance. Never try to say something funny about an embarrassing situation. Remember that everybody has bad breath once in a while, although he or she doesn't always know it. Use yourself as an example. Say his breath is really strong and that when yours has been that way you started using mouthwash or brushing your teeth more often. You might even discuss which brands are good.

This really will be a test of your friendship, because you risk making him angry and defensive, but being friends means more than sticking around for the laughs. It means being honest with the people you care about. Sooner or later he will realize that you were trying to help, not hurt.

Q. ***My friend talks all the time. She never shuts up. Nobody else gets a chance to talk around her. What should we do?***

A. Avoid cruel hints. Don't present your friend with a tube of Krazy Glue for her mouth. Don't whip out earplugs when you see her coming. There is a chatterbox in every crowd, a fact of life that never changes. In this situation you should support your friend while preserving other friendships.

Try saying "Look, it isn't fair that you just talk all the time and never get to listen to anybody else. When you talk nonstop, none of us get to share anything in our lives. We'd all be happier if you would give us equal time and listen to us. It is important that we all get along." Remember to say this in private. Be calm, not combative or accusatory. What you want to get is a give-and-take friendship, not an argument. Rehearse what you plan to say when you're alone in your room. Do it in front of a mirror. Do your best to control your tone of voice to spare your friend's feelings and reduce the chances of getting tongue-tied and end up feeling like a jerk.

Q. ***If you are on the bus and somebody next to you smells, what should you do?***

A. Move! And if that isn't possible, do your best to turn away from the person as unobtrusively as possible and change your seat as soon as you can. Don't gasp for breath, fake a faint, or make a face mask out of your scarf. That will accomplish nothing except embarrass the offending person and make you look like a moron.

Even if you know the person, don't say anything during the

bus ride. Nothing can be done to correct the problem at that moment. Others might hear you, which would be humiliating to that person. Nobody deserves humiliation. If you are a friend, do this person a favor and explain quietly and privately later. That way, the person can fix the problem and won't offend anyone else or be embarrassed.

Q. ***I think my friend is an alcoholic. She thinks it's fun to play with her parents' whiskey because they drink all the time. I think she has some in her locker at school. What should I do?***

A. If your friend is an alcoholic, she probably wouldn't want to hear about it from you. That should not stop you from telling her that you worry about her, however. Drinking alcohol can be dangerous, especially at a young age. Please remember that there is very little you can do other than remain her friend and continue to care. Tell your parents what you've told me. They will be in a better position to go through the appropriate channels. Your friend's parents may not be helpful. Ask your parents to research some programs that you can attend about teen alcoholism. This is a more widespread problem than you might think. Good luck. You're a great friend.

Punctuality

Q. ***My friend is always late when we meet at the movies. She gets mad if I go in without her, but I get mad if I don't get to see the beginning. Is it wrong for me to go in and not wait for her?***

A. Being late even once is bad manners, period. Being late all the time is more than impolite; it shows disrespect for your feelings, your friendship, and your valuable time. Tell your friend that the next time she is late, you plan to go in and see the movie from the start. Sometimes we can't control things like buses being on time, so it is considerate to wait fifteen minutes when your plans are casual, like having a snack together. The really important thing is that you and your friends keep your agreements with each other.

Q. ***Last Saturday, I forgot to meet my friend at the movies because my mom and I went to the mall and stayed late. She was really mad and now won't speak to me. What's the best way to apologize so she will believe that I'm sorry and didn't mean it?***

A. Of course she's angry. Wouldn't you be? All of us have done this at one time or another. If I were you, I would go to her house and apologize. Take a gift, especially if you can make it yourself, like her favorite cookies or brownies. Try flowers if you don't cook. A single beautiful tulip, rose, or carnation shouldn't hurt your budget too much. Spend some time making sure that your gift is wrapped nicely and that you arrive looking your best. Wearing your best outfit is not necessary; just demonstrate through your appearance that she is important to you.

When you talk to her, look her in the eye, tell her you would never deliberately hurt her for anything in the world, and say that you certainly can understand why she is so angry. Above all, don't blame your absence on anyone else. Own up to forgetting. Take responsibility. Don't pass the blame. She surely will forgive you—and perhaps learn something from you if it ever happens to her.

Q. ***I'm always the first one to arrive at parties because my mom says it's important to be on time. But it is really embarrassing. What should I do?***

A. Well, you can't evaporate until the rest of the guests arrive, but you can learn to be at ease on your own. I promise it will get easier. First, introduce yourself to your friend's parents if you don't already know them. If it is a birthday party, present your gift when you arrive. Tell your host how pleased you are to be there. If you are alone for a while, ask if there is anything you can do to help. That should break the ice. Then you can talk about school, movies, clothes, or whatever.

It is true that there is safety in numbers, especially at parties. Next time you might want to arrange to meet another friend who is also invited and go together.

Your mom is right about not being late. Just don't show up so early that you throw the host into a panic because the party isn't ready, even if it means walking around the block a time or two to delay your entrance closer to the time the party is supposed to begin.

Respect

Q. ***What do you do when a friend makes fun of something very important to you?***

A. Most of the time such show-offs want to be in the spotlight, whatever the cost. They need to draw attention to themselves. Dealing with them is tough and requires patience. For starters, remember that there is strength in silence. If you are in a group of people and this person persists on making fun of something important, you can simply be silent instead of laughing with the others. You would be surprised at how much attention you

---

There is no such thing as a popular bully.

---

will get then. Someone probably will try to ask why you are not responding. That's when you can say that you don't find the person's jokes funny.

If this kind of behavior continues, you don't have to be a party to it. Get up and walk away. If people ask why, tell them. If, on the other hand, someone is teasing you about something that's important to you, don't just sit there and be a wimp. Be honest and direct. Tell the person the joke is hurtful because the topic is important to you. Ask the person to respect your feelings. If it doesn't stop, quietly excuse yourself and leave.

Q. ***How should I act when my friend is rude to somebody in my family all the time?***

A. If you have tried everything (including plainly but privately telling your friend how much her conduct hurts and embarrasses you) and the rudeness continues, perhaps it is time to find a new friend. Do you really want to be friends with someone like that? Maybe not. As the old saying goes, with friends like that, who needs enemies?

Saying "no problem" is never the same as saying "you're welcome."

Q. ***Why do I have to be polite to friends?***

A. Being polite simply means that you are considerate of your friends' feelings. That's always important, whether you're dealing with friends or strangers. A friend is somebody you care about more than other people because you share the same likes and dislikes. When we know a person well, we naturally tend to become much more relaxed and less formal. Because you know a friend well, the way to be polite in his or her company may be different from the way you are polite to strangers. For example, we often tease friends. In that case being polite means knowing when to stop before you hurt your friend's feelings. The basic rules apply. Taking a friend for granted is a sure way to lose one.

Walk away from bullies. Then shake the dust from your shoes.

Q. ***My friend is always mean to my dog when she comes over. What should I do?***

A. Abuse to animals should not be tolerated anywhere, especially in your own home to your own pet. It is usually a bully who picks on people or innocent animals who can't fight back. By all means, tell your friend not to be mean to your dog. If she persists, protest loudly and don't invite her back. Ask yourself if this is really the kind of friend you want. You don't have to apologize or be shy about saying "Listen, why don't you pick on somebody your own size? This is my dog's home, too."

Shyness

Q. ***I'm sometimes shy with new people. Is there anything I can do about it?***

A. I find meeting new people extremely challenging myself. I've trained myself over the years to make it look easy. You can, too. We are in good company. Some of the most famous actors and actresses turned to the stage or screen to overcome shyness. Their strong desire to conquer their shortcoming propelled them to greatness. These people include Barbra Streisand and Holly Hunter.

A good thing to keep in mind is that most people are genuinely curious. Upon meeting someone new they want to know who they are, where they live, and what they do. One great way to overcome shyness is to introduce yourself to somebody in the crowd who obviously is not shy. Take a deep breath. Tell yourself, "I can do this." Make eye contact. Put out your hand and say, "Hi, I'm Kathryn." You're sure to get a response and handshake back.

Energy and enthusiasm are magnets for new friends.

You can always get the conversation started after the introductions by saying things like "I couldn't help noticing what a great sweater you're wearing" and "I go to Kennedy High School. What school do you attend?" The answers will lead to other questions about people you both may know, fashions, sports, hobbies, or other activities. It is a good idea to give some information about yourself and then lead into a question. It also is a good idea to avoid questions that have yes-or-no, one-word answers that can stop a conversation cold.

If you pay attention, people will give you clues about themselves that can keep the conversation going. For example, if a person is carrying a bicycle helmet or a tennis racket, you probably can get a conversation going about cycling or tennis. Practice making up questions like these when you're alone so that they come easily to you when you're meeting new people. Remember, very few people are truly at ease around strangers. Practice these skills, take some risks, and you'll end up winning new friends. Go for it.

Everybody's shy sometimes.
But all of us can overcome it.

Q. ***I never like talking to my parents. What can I do to start talking to them? Every time I go to church or somewhere new I seem too shy. But in school I never seem too shy. I'm always talking to my friends. What can I do to stop being so shy?***

A. If you've ever watched the Olympics, you saw some great ways to overcome shyness. Athletes push themselves beyond what they believe their physical limits are and they go on to break new ground—for themselves and for others. And if you ask a fine athlete what makes it possible to do that, often the answer is "preparation." Not only the physical practice, but the mental practice—going over and over a race in his or her mind, time and time again, anticipating any difficult patches, and figuring out how to deal with them. By the time the race actually occurs, the athlete is ready, excited, and feels somewhat familiar with the course.

Why not approach your shyness in much the same way? You said that you have no difficulty talking with your schoolmates. Probably the reason is that they are all very familiar to you and you share the same experiences every day. It's different with new people or people you see only once in a while. So prepare for meeting these new people as though you were an athlete preparing for a major race or game. Give yourself the gift of good preparation. What do you expect to happen? How large a crowd will be there? What exactly is the event—a party, a church service, a game, or a dance? What will you wear? How do you want to look? Go ahead and write down your answers. Then write down for yourself—nobody ever has to see it—a list of good things about yourself. Maybe you really like your hair, or you have great eyes, or you know you have a great sense of humor that nobody knows about. Maybe you know a lot about soccer or a certain kind of music. Put those things on your list; it'll make you feel good about yourself and boost your confidence. Next make a list of some things you can talk about. You can get ideas from magazines, radio, television, or the newspaper. Think about those things. Now imagine yourself actually at the event. Close your eyes and try to see yourself there, how you'll look, and imagine yourself laughing and talking with people. Imagine yourself seeing somebody there just as shy as you are and walking up to that person and starting a conversation. You can say something as straightforward and honest as, "I noticed that you don't seem to know a lot of people here, either. My name is __________." You'll seem like a real hero to another shy person—and best of all, you'll be your own hero once you do that.

Overcoming shyness doesn't mean you become the life of the party in one day. Start with small steps. Talk to just one new person at a time. Gradually you'll get used to doing it, and while you might never find it easy, I guarantee that if you do your homework, you will get better at it and you'll feel much better about yourself.

I have found that the best way to be a good conversationalist is to be a good listener. Maybe you can test your listening skills on your parents. Try asking them whether they ever felt shy and listen to what they tell you. Sometimes we think we have trouble talking to people, when what's really going on is that we have trouble listening to them. And remember that, just as an athlete celebrates winning—or a new personal best—you have every right to congratulate yourself on every single "overcoming shyness" victory—no matter how tiny.

Siblings

Q. ***Sometimes the girlfriends I invite to my house want to play with my older brother instead of me. It makes me feel sad and mad. What should I do?***

A. Unfortunately, a good hostess really can't dictate how guests behave or how they want to play. But every good hostess plans how she entertains, so there are a couple of things you can do to avoid this problem.

First, you can negotiate with your brother; convince him to disappear when your friends come over. You also can find out from him or your mother when he'll be out of the house so that you can ask your friends over then. I think it is important to tell him that it makes you feel sad and mad when you have to share your friends. Ask him to help you. Remind him that, in a few years, his friends might want to spend time with you and that you will understand if that also would make him sad or mad. Don't try to lock him in his room and tell your friends that he was sent away for acting like an older brother . . . even if you really want to.

Q. ***My sister is very weird. When we are in public, I pretend she isn't my sister. What can I do?***

A. I'm not exactly sure what you mean by weird, but I am sure that you are embarrassed by your sister when you have to associate with her in public. Remember the old saying "You can pick your friends but not your family." Since she is your sister, you have a better opportunity than most people to find some time alone with her to talk. Make it just between the two of you.

Nobody likes to be judged, so don't do it. Just tell her directly that when she acts in certain ways she embarrasses you. You'll have to explain exactly what you mean; be prepared to be specific. Saying "You act weird" is too general to be helpful. And once you've said it, don't nag. If she pays attention, you will have spared her future embarrassment.

However, there always is the possibility that she is simply radically different and sees things very differently from you. Many popular people capitalize on their weirdness. Look at popular rock music figures. They might seem weird to us, but they sure have made the world a more interesting place. If this is the case, the best thing you can do is appreciate her uniqueness and support it. Trying to change people never works and always produces hard feelings.

Sports

Q. ***My friend and I are on the same basketball team. She's a real ball hog. She's the best player we have, but she never passes even though somebody else may have a better shot. We've lost the last two games. How do I tell her without hurting her feelings or sounding like I'm jealous?***

A. Even famous athletes are the first to admit they need a team around them to be successful. Let's examine the key characteristics of a winning team:

The goal is to win the game. To do that, all team members must be in accord. They don't necessarily have to agree on everything, but when the action starts they have to work and move as a unit toward the common goal. In your team's situation this means recognizing that whoever has the clear shot should have the ball. True team players support their team members, another essential ingredient in winning. That means each player recognizes the strengths and weaknesses of the other individuals and gives help—or asks for help—when needed. Finally (and this often is the toughest skill to master), team players must trust each other. You have to trust each player to perform to his or her best possible ability.

We aren't all born team players. Most of us have to learn those lessons over time, often the hard way—by losing an important game. So remember that your friend probably sees the situation differently. She probably is just charging in, doing what she thinks is the best way to get the job done. Maybe she even feels as if the recent losses are entirely her fault and is trying single-handedly to make up for them.

Play fair; don't change the rules to win the game.

Get her alone and be honest. Let her know that you recognize how talented she is and that you sometimes feel you don't get a chance to contribute. Tell her everybody on the team is capable of doing something to help the team win. Add that if she would just use those other team-member skills, she might be able to concentrate on her strengths while others on the team would have the opportunity to contribute and, more important, share in the final score. Your friend might not change her behavior, but she will have something to think about the next time your team falls behind.

Tact and Diplomacy

Q. ***How do I get my friend to leave when he has stayed at my house long enough?***

A. You should be tactful. After all, you can't throw a friend out just because you're no longer amused by his or her company, especially since you extended the invitation in the first place. Honesty is the best policy here, but remember to use tact (the ability to do and say the right thing when dealing with people, particularly in difficult situations).

Doing the right thing means not hurting your friend's feelings. A good friend will understand if you say "I have homework to do" or "I need to get some rest." One good way to avoid this sticky situation altogether is by giving your friend an idea in advance of how long you would like him to stay. You can invite him over for the morning, afternoon, or evening and add that you're looking forward to seeing him even though the rest of your day is somewhat full with studies, family activities, or whatever. It is not fair to let a friend think he's invited for a long time and then tell him he has to go before that time is up, unless something unexpected comes up or he is acting mean or rude. In those cases, tell him the reason you're asking him to leave, again using tact and honesty.

Gossip or tell a secret, and you're likely to lose a friend's trust forever.

Q. ***What do you do when your friend has a new outfit and asks your opinion and you dislike it? Do you lie or tell the truth?***

A. Don't lie, but to spare your friend's feelings you must tell the truth in a very sensitive manner. For example, you could say something like "Well, it's very nice, but I've seen colors that look better on you." Approaching the answer this way honors your friend with honest feedback because you've taken the time to pay attention to the details and communicate your observations.

Q. ***How do you tell a friend to butt out of other people's business?***

A. Curiosity, the need or desire to know something, is a condition that almost everyone is born with. Many people look first at the gossip column of a newspaper or magazine. Some of the largest publications in the world are devoted to printing the details and dramas of "other people's business." It is human nature to be curious.

With this in mind, avoiding or quieting prying questions is difficult. It seems that the more you don't tell someone, the more he or she wants to know. However, you can handle an overly curious person in a few ways. Here are some examples:

"That's really a family matter, and we don't want to talk about it in public."

"It's a personal thing, so let's leave it alone."

"Please don't ask about that anymore because it hurts to talk about it."

"Talk like that might hurt some people, so please drop the subject."

As I said, people love to gossip. Your request may be ignored. If you make your statement strongly, seriously, and without anger, however, it's likely the person you're telling will listen and act accordingly.

6
Table Manners

"Manners are your station in life."
Eugene F. Brussel

For parents . . .

I was catching a quick dinner at a neighborhood Chinese restaurant and couldn't help noticing in the small, crowded room a table of three young gentlemen having dinner. They appeared to be about eleven or twelve years old. They caught my eye because they were having such a wonderful time. They were laughing, talking, and sharing food without offending other diners.

Because of their nice grooming and polite demeanor, I half expected a parent or another adult to walk in and occupy the fourth seat. My dinner arrived, but again and again my attention was diverted to those kids and what a good time they were having. No adults arrived. There wasn't a supervisor at another table. They were on their own.

By the look of it, no adult supervision was needed. Their napkins were on their laps. They sat up in their chairs. They passed and shared food from three large dishes placed in the center of the table. They laughed throughout the entire meal without a single food fight. When one talked, the other two listened and didn't interrupt. At one point they needed a water refill. They didn't raise their hands or shout across the room. Instead they waited patiently for a moment, made eye contact with their server, and, when he came to the table, asked for water.

Extraordinary? You bet. But it didn't end there. When the bill arrived, they collectively counted out their money, calculated the tip, thanked the server, and left. As a restaurant veteran and observer of human behavior, I was delighted and flabbergasted by those fellows. How many times have you seen supposedly sophisticated adults call across the room for their servers, get more food on their faces than in their mouths, interrupt loudly when somebody is trying to finish a sentence, and become almost combative when settling a bill three ways?

I wish I knew their parents. I would tell them what an outstanding job they had done—and not just because their children knew what to do with their napkins and utensils. Plenty of kids know the rules and use them when they have to. The most outstanding thing their parents did was to instill in their children the understanding that good table manners and correct etiquette are not something to haul out wearily only when an adult is present. If anything, the rules are there to make good times better. They are based on respect, kindness, and consideration. What could be better than that? I salute parents who instill this understanding in their children and who know what a dining experience should be—sharing good food, good conversation, and good friends with good manners.

Conversely, isn't it one of every parent's worst nightmares to raise a child who is clueless about how to behave—and gains a reputation for it that follows the child forever?

There are, of course, worse fates in life than not knowing which fork to use. But there are few things most of us fear more than being unable to earn a living because we never learned to function productively in our work and social arenas. More business than ever is being conducted at the dining table today. The trend will escalate as our economy becomes more global and as we accede to the customs of other countries that place high regard on the "ceremony" of dining.

Formal, multicourse meals are becoming something of a dinosaur, but that does not mean that fast food is the norm or that fast-food table manners are the yardstick. We set up our children for failure if we do not teach them how to dine. Peanut butter on their T-shirts today can mean disappointment tomorrow. Just as nobody ever learned to ride a bike by reading a book, nobody ever learned table manners from a lecture. Good manners are the ultimate hands-on learning experience. Parents must set the example. Children are great mimics. They learn best through immersion and osmosis.

I am a realist. I am not suggesting you turn your home life into a series of gracious "Leave It to Beaver" reruns. Today's reality is that, in most families, both parents work, life is generally more expensive, and even children have grueling schedules. What I am suggesting is this:

Learn good table manners. Use them in front of your children. Recognize that these lessons are a matter of continuing exposure; nobody is at ease in a first-time situation.

If you don't, you cannot expect your child to perform well at his or her first important mealtime interview. It could be a college entrance meeting, a first job interview, or that unnerving introductory experience with the parents of a romantic interest. In any of these situations you cannot expect flawless results from a child who spends more time worrying about what to do with a linen napkin than acting naturally and comfortably.

The good news here is that we are not talking about learning brain surgery. Mastering dining etiquette requires only a simple awareness of the basics and a good role model. At home or in a restaurant, table manners are the same.

If you would like a head start before you begin to teach your children, read the following list. I've observed these to be the most common dining etiquette mistakes.

1. Misusing silverware: I don't mean using the wrong implement but using any implement incorrectly. This is the most common mistake and the easiest to make. The "cello grasp" is the major mistake with a fork. The "dagger grip" with a knife is second. Other mistakes include resting silverware on the table or at the edge of a plate (one slip and you have a mess), leaving a knife blade facing outward on a plate and waving cutlery in the air to make a point. There is one basic silverware rule: once you pick it up, it should never again touch the table.

2. Poor posture: Food doesn't go down as well, and, frankly, you're not as attractive to those around you at the table when you're in a slump. Sit straight. You'll actually be more comfortable.

3. Talking with a full mouth: The corollary is chewing with your mouth open. If your mouth has food in it, keep it closed. Take small bites. Finish chewing. Smile and only then carry on your part of the conversation.

4. Not breaking bread: A quick indicator to all of whether you know basic table manners. Do not butter an entire roll or slice of bread and then cut it with a knife. Bread and rolls served with meals are meant to be broken with the fingers and buttered one piece at a time. "Breaking bread" is a throwback to times when uneaten food was distributed to the poor. A person never broke off more from the communal loaf than he or she could eat.

5. Leaving lipstick stains: A more modern problem, and bad form, particularly for women in the business arena. Don't leave makeup stains on glasses or cups. Cosmetics should be put on your face to stay. They are esthetically unpleasant anywhere else. If you do not carry tissues with you, make a quick detour to the powder room for tissue or to the bar for a paper cocktail napkin to blot with.

6. Eating/dining too fast: It doesn't matter if you're at McDonald's or The Ritz-Carlton. Gulping food is bad for your digestion and unattractive to those around you. Dining is not a solo experience. What you do individually affects everyone at the table. When eating with others, everyone should have the same number of courses and start and finish each at approximately the same pace.

7. Misusing a napkin: A napkin should be used to carefully dab the corners of the mouth. It is not a blotter or a flag. Open your napkin and spread it across your lap during the meal. Leave it there until the meal is concluded. If you leave the table temporarily, leave the napkin on your chair and slide the chair under the table. The reason is that it's pretty gross to look at somebody's food residue when you're in the middle of the meal. It's also not sanitary to put all those germs on the table for other diners to catch.

8. Putting items on the table: Purses, briefcases, keys, hats, gloves—anything that is not part of the meal—do not belong on the table. It is unsightly and unsanitary.

If all else fails, remember that courtesy, kindness, and common sense can get you through most dining experiences.

Remember too that there are styles of dining other than American. Familiarize yourself with the continental (or European) style (see Chapter 10). Children will learn this style more quickly than adults. They don't have preconceived biases. Continental dining used to be snickered at as "affected." Today it is enjoying the popularity it deserves. It is much simpler, more elegant, and more efficient. At the very least it is important to recognize continental dining so that your children will become comfortable with it.

It also is very helpful for parents to learn and understand the "anatomy" of a restaurant—how it works and who does what—to be able to lead properly by example when dining out with the family (see also Chapter 10).

Where to start? Try the following list of dining etiquette questions asked most often by an audience of American children, aged eight to fifteen:

Beverages

Q. ***How should you drink milk, orange juice, and grape juice without getting a mustache?***

A. Carefully and slowly. Sipping instead of gulping is the only way. Try practicing.

Burping

Q. ***What do I do when I can tell that I'm going to burp or break wind and there are people around?***

A. At one time or another this happens to all of us. It doesn't get any less embarrassing as you get older. Usually you really do know in time to excuse yourself from the table or gathering, so don't hang around trying to make a photo finish of it. If the offensive sound does occur, don't make a big deal out of it. Just say "Excuse me" to no one in particular. Believe me, everyone else will be embarrassed for you and will help you put the event in the past.

Bread Plates

Q. ***Whenever I'm at a round table, I don't know which side my bread plate is on. What's the answer?***

A. Your bread plate is always to your left, regardless of the shape of the table. When someone commandeers your bread plate, just use your dinner plate instead of creating another mistake destined to confuse somebody else.

Break off one bite-size piece of bread at a time, butter it, and eat it. Never butter a whole slice.

Clothing

Q. ***Is it rude to wear a hat to dinner?***

A. For young gentlemen, hats at dinner and anyplace else indoors (except at a sporting event) are just not cool. Like coats, hats are made to be worn outdoors to protect you from the elements, the sun and the cold. You can wear your hat at an outdoor picnic dinner, but never inside. In fact the mark of a gentleman is that he always removes his hat indoors. Although baseball caps are worn everywhere today, they really aren't accepted in more conservative places such as churches, nice restaurants, theaters, and people's homes. I know of school officials around the country who are saying no to anybody who wants to wear a hat indoors, regardless of gender.

For young ladies it is entirely appropriate to wear hats

indoors at meals. It looks quite elegant. This happens naturally more at lunch than at dinner. In the business arena today, women are wearing hats indoors and outdoors less and less so that they don't detract from their professional credibility by appearing frilly. At the same time, men are keeping their hats on in elevators, which only a few years ago was a no-no.

In contemporary times, logic suggests that the reason women keep their hats on indoors is that removing them creates or reveals a bad-hair day. This usually is not the case with men. Hats were an important part of a man's wardrobe until about thirty-five years ago, when President John F. Kennedy stopped wearing them after his inauguration.

In primitive history, head coverings of some sort came about before other clothing. In Western civilizations, people built shelters before they made clothes for the body.

A *haet* or *hutt* shielded them from rain, snow, wind, and darkness. Later, when they made something they could wear around to protect their heads from weather or falling debris, this head covering carried the same name, *haet* or *hutt.*

In classical times, women hardly ever wore hats, and men kept theirs on indoors and in churches and cathedrals. Those customs continued until the 1500s, when huge, cumbersome wigs became the fashion and wearing hats became difficult at best for men. Once wearing wigs lost popularity, men went back to wearing hats, although with less enthusiasm. In fact, customs were reversed: men never wore hats indoors, in church, or in the presence of a woman.

Some people of both sexes wear hats indoors because of their religion. This is always appropriate. Thus, an etiquette rule should come second to personal religious beliefs.

Company

Q. *Why is it that, every time people come for dinner, I have to eat differently?*

A. Most people's manners slip when they're with only their families. Their manners improve when guests are around. If all members of your family eat with their feet and elbows on the table and their faces in their plates, then that's the norm. It's what you have become used to.

However, since the beginning of time, guests in one's home have been given a place of honor and other special treatment. That means the guests usually get the best food and the best seats at the table. Likewise, it is customary to show one's best manners so guests are comfortable and feel special and welcome. Not doing so shows a lack of respect for your guests.

Q. *When people are eating sloppily, should you tell them?*

A. The big question here is "When is it our place to correct someone who is being rude?" There is no easy answer, for adults as well as for kids. If your friend is sitting next to you in the cafeteria and chowing down like Orca the Killer Whale on a feeding frenzy, it is OK to tell him he's embarrassing himself and others. You can say "Hey, buddy, there's food all over your face, you sound like a vacuum cleaner, and you just ruined your shirt."

Risky as that is, you can say it if he's your friend. A true friend will appreciate the tip, although he may get angry for the moment.

It is not, however, your place to correct the eating habits of strangers. When you accidentally end up with Sid Slob, a complete stranger, as a dining companion, you have only one option: chalk it up to experience and set a good example yourself.

Q. *Why can't we eat with our hands when guests come to dinner?*

A. Well, we can. It depends on what we're eating. Ribs and pizza are fine to eat with the hands. And imagine trying to eat corn on the cob with a knife and fork or a pair of chopsticks.

However, in today's world other foods require appropriate tools. It is pretty hard to eat soup without a spoon or to eat a grilled steak with your hands and not have to change into clean clothes afterward, for example. That's why knives, forks, and chopsticks were invented and why we use them.

When forks first appeared in Italy about nine hundred years ago, they were not widely accepted. People at that time still preferred to use their fingers and a knife. Forks became popular only about two hundred years ago. However, not all cultures embraced the newfangled invention. In the Middle East and parts of Africa, for example, people still eat properly with their hands. The food of those cultures is designed to be eaten that way.

The best rule here is to go by the old saying "When in Rome, do as the Romans do." Adopt the customs of the culture you are in. If you happened to find yourself dining with a family of baboons, it would even be proper to eat with your feet.

Q. *Why can't guests clean up the table after dinner?*

A. Guests can clean up the table, but a host who would like help will not ask for it unless the guest offers first. It is not a good idea to invite somebody to your home expecting the visitor to clean it for you. Whether a guest is a friend or a stranger, a good host makes sure a guest's wishes and needs are cared for.

On the other hand, if your best friend is at your house for dinner five nights a week, he or she has become somewhat of a family fixture and should be expected to help out. If that's the case, it is all right to ask your friend for some assistance.

Q. ***Should you help clean up dishes at a friend's house?***

A. In almost any situation it is important to offer your help and be willing to help, whether it is at a dinner or a picnic. The offer is almost more important than the deed. Sometimes the host might not want your help. It might be simpler for him or her to do it alone. Or the host might want you to relax and enjoy being a guest. In this case it is the thought that counts.

Q. ***Is it rude to eat before everyone is seated?***

A. Absolutely. Mealtime is a time not only to eat but also to share yourself and your company with friends and family. If you eat before everyone is there, it is a clear sign that you are not willing to share. I know that a few minutes spent waiting for others to arrive at the table often seems like an eternity—but hang on. You can make it. If the offenders are family members, you might try to round them up just before the meal so you all get there at the same time and nobody has to wait.

Q. ***Do we have to eat things we don't like in front of our guests?***

A. I know it doesn't do much for the appetite to be served food we don't like—especially when there are guests in our home and we are on our best behavior to make them feel comfortable. Think about how you would feel if you had prepared a meal for someone and your own family members would not eat it. I bet your feelings would be hurt, and chances are you would be pretty irritated to have your cooking efforts rebuffed. Nobody likes rejection, so when you are served something you don't like, do not roll your eyes, make a face, and sigh. Instead of showing displeasure, eat at least a little bit of everything you are served.

You don't have to eat all of it. Move around on your plate the food you don't like so that it looks as if you are eating it. This is a good skill to learn as early as you can. It has been my experience that this situation never stops coming up. It is more important to understand that it makes a guest feel uncomfortable to be invited into an atmosphere that isn't harmonious. Causing discord by criticizing the hosts—even if they are your parents—just isn't playing fair. In the end, you're the one who looks bad because you're being rude to the hosts and guests both.

Q. ***My girlfriend always eats from my plate, and it drives me crazy. It doesn't seem to matter if we have exactly the same thing. How do I get her to stop?***

A. You're perfectly entitled to be irritated. It's not good manners or good hygiene. Avoid the problem before it arises. Offer her some of your food before she dives in. If she says yes, cut some off and put it on the side of her plate or on her bread plate.

Have you told her how nuts it makes you, or are you suffering in silence? You might have to make your point more than once, but eventually she will get the message. What happens if you do the same to her food? Does she try to impale your wrist with a fork, or is she willing to share? Good communication and observing etiquette rules should salvage your sanity in this situation.

Conversation

Q. ***What do you talk about over a meal?***

A. That depends on the company and what you have in common. The list of dinner conversation topics is endless. To name a few: Sports, events of the day, movies, school, friends, television programs, and music.

In general, the easiest way to get a conversation going is to ask questions—and listen to the answers. Ask what somebody did that day, for example. Perhaps there is a newcomer at dinner or lunch, a friend of somebody in your family. Ask how they met. People really appreciate knowing that you are interested in them, whether they are adults or kids. That's why it is really important to show you're listening. Think about how important you feel when somebody takes the time to find out what your favorite sport, movie, or music is.

Don't ask somebody a question you wouldn't want anybody to ask you. Mealtimes are meant for sharing ourselves, our experiences, and our friends and family. They should be pleasant times. Steer clear of unpleasant topics like what you dissected in biology class or somebody's disease or divorce.

Never ask a question you wouldn't want to answer yourself.

Q. ***If you didn't have a good meal, should you say you did?***

A. There's no reason to hurt someone with the brutal truth, but you don't have to lie either. If you are a guest in a friend's home or at a restaurant, you can always find something nice to say about the food. For example: "Thank you. I never had snails before."

Remember, if you are a guest, any food prepared for you is a gift. That's true at home as well. If you have a friend to dinner at your house and dinner isn't quite what you'd hoped for, you shouldn't say anything. It will only embarrass your friend and whoever cooked the food. That is very bad manners.

Food is not the only thing that makes a good meal. The fact that someone invited you or prepared a meal for you can make even the most dismal dinner a great feast.

Q. ***My mom always tells me to use good manners, but my uncle curses and never says please or thank you at the dinner table. What should I do?***

A. Set a good example, and maybe your uncle will learn a lesson from it. The truth is that adults with bad manners generally are not liked. They usually are not very successful because nobody really wants to be around them. Listen to your mom and remember that it is not your place to correct your uncle. But it is your place to use good manners.

Doggie Bags

Q. ***Sometimes when I eat in a restaurant, I can't finish all the food. Is it rude to ask for a doggie bag?***

A. You don't always see doggie bags in fancy restaurants, but they're gradually increasing in popularity. In less formal restaurants, requests for doggie bags are a frequent occurrence. Usually the waiter will ask if you would like to have the remainder of your food wrapped. If he doesn't, then it is perfectly fine to ask "Would it be possible to take this home with me?"

The practice of taking doggie bags home is not accepted in all cultures but it's acceptable in the United States.

Dropped or Lost Items

Q. *What do I do when I drop something on the floor during a meal?*

A. It makes a difference whether you're at home, at a friend's, or at a restaurant.

At home, of course, it is expected and proper to pick up whatever you've dropped and dispose of it. Be sure to ask to be excused when you leave the table to handle the matter. No fair "accidentally" dropping food for your dog.

If you are at a friend's house and a piece of your roll slides under the table, just leave it there until you've finished and then pick it up. That way you won't disrupt the meal.

All of us occasionally drop a fork or knife in a restaurant. Leave whatever you dropped on the floor and ask your host to ask the waiter to replace it. Be sure to thank the waiter when he does so, as well as your host.

Q. *What happens if you lose your tooth or shoe at the table?*

A. Two lost items, two solutions.

"Grin and bear it" is not exactly the case with your lost tooth, but almost. There's nothing wrong with losing a tooth at the table, so don't be embarrassed. But don't embarrass yourself by making a grand announcement. If you have to search for the lost tooth, ask to be excused from the table and take care of it. Don't bring the specimen back to the table for a group inspection. If you do leave the table, remember to leave your napkin (which probably is bloodstained) on the chair and not on the table.

Losing one's shoe at the table is quite another story. It's hardly a medical emergency, but we're supposed to remain fully clothed during meals. Don't suddenly slide under the table in search of your lost shoe. Nobody knows you've lost it. Instead, wait until the meal is over to retrieve it. You can do this most naturally when everybody is walking away from the table. If you do have to leave the table before the end of the meal, get up out of your chair and apologize to your dining neighbors that you're on a shoe reconnaissance mission. This happens to all of us at one time or another.

Finger Foods

Q. ***Are there any foods that are appropriate to eat with your fingers?***

A. Some foods only taste right when you eat them with your fingers, such as fried chicken, pizza, spareribs, and french fries. They're meant to be eaten with your fingers when you're with family and friends, at a home or a fast-food restaurant. You probably won't find these things served at a formal restaurant or meal, but if you do, make your best effort with a knife and fork.

You're more likely to be served steamed artichokes or asparagus at a fancier setting. Those also are eaten with the fingers (as long as the asparagus isn't dripping with sauce). Olives are eaten with the fingers no matter where you are.

Q. ***How do you eat corn on the cob? I think it makes sense to butter a piece of bread and then spread it on the corn.***

A. It makes sense until the bread falls apart and you are left with a mess on your hands (and probably down your arms).

The idea of eating corn properly is to have the best time you can with the least mess. Try spreading butter on just a couple of rows at a time, then adding salt and pepper if you use them. When you have eaten those rows, butter the next two, and so on. That way the butter doesn't end up all over you and your clothes.

Q. ***How do I eat an artichoke?***

A. Patiently and carefully. They really are a lot of effort for not very much result, but they taste great if you like them. Once you get the hang of it, they're easy to eat.

The good news is that artichokes are eaten with the fingers. Take off one leaf at a time. Dip the soft end in the sauce and then pull it through your teeth. The edible part will come off. Discard the rest. Use your knife to scrape the fuzzy stuff (the stuff that looks like it would choke you) off the fleshy part in the center, called the *heart.* Eat the heart with your knife and fork. You can dip the pieces into your sauce after they're on your fork. Be sure to use your napkin often to wipe the sauce from the corners of your mouth and fingers.

Finishing Meals

Q. ***What do you do when you go out to eat and you cannot finish your food? Is it rude to leave it there?***

A. It isn't always rude to leave food on your plate, but it is bad manners to waste food. Let's take a look at some situations:

In a restaurant, we don't know how much food we're going to be served or how it will taste. We just might not be able to finish the portions we're given. There's nothing worse than feeling ill—or getting sick—because you've overeaten or eaten something that isn't right. In a restaurant it is easy (and perfectly good manners) to ask for a doggie bag. That way you or someone else, or even the doggie, can enjoy it later.

Cover your mouth when you yawn.

When you're at someone's home and you're helping yourself, never take more than you know you can eat. Remember to leave plenty for other people sharing the meal. Serving yourself too much food is rude and discourteous.

One more thing to remember: finishing a large portion is not an excuse to announce that you're stuffed and feeling like a blimp in Macy's Thanksgiving Day Parade. Just put your knife and fork down and tell your host you enjoyed the meal.

Gifts

Q. ***My mom says I should always take a gift when I go to someone's house for dinner. Is this true? If bringing a gift is really good manners, what kind of gift should I give?***

A. Your mother is right on this one. It is very good manners to bring a small hostess gift when you go to someone's house for dinner. Your gift should be simple and small. Be sure to wrap it beautifully to show you paid attention and cared enough to present your gift well, which requires thought and time. The most important thing to remember about bringing a hostess gift is to avoid anything that might distract your hostess from her chores to attend to your gift. For example, a bouquet of freshly cut flowers is beautiful but would require her to stop what she's doing, find a vase, and arrange them. That can be troublesome if dinner might also be burning on the stove. Also avoid gifts that should be eaten at the meal. It might upset your hostess's plan. If you've brought brownies or made cookies, give them in a sealed tin and say something like "I thought you might like these for the weekend." Small books always are appropriate and appreciated. So are lovely paper napkins, candy, and fine nuts. Plants also are nice because they remind us of the person who gave them as they grow.

Invitations

Q. ***If you're invited to dinner and you don't want to go, how do you say no?***

A. Not an easy question to answer. It is a position you'll find yourself in many times throughout your life.

If it is a really important occasion and not being there would hurt somebody, you should go. It's not going to kill you. From time to time we all have to do things that don't thrill us.

If, however, the event isn't especially significant, reply simply and straightforwardly. Say something like "Sorry. I won't be able to come over, but thanks a lot for the invitation. Maybe another time." You can tell the truth without being hurtful.

Makeup

Q. ***Why do girls have to go to the ladies' room to put on makeup at a restaurant?***

A. Why in the world would you want to show everybody all it takes to complete the look? For one thing, applying makeup in public certainly takes away whatever mystique surrounds how and why you look so good. More important, mealtimes are not cosmetic commercials. You should come to the table dressed and made up (if you wear makeup) because meals are times to share your company, conversation, and ideas, not your toilette.

The only thing that might need repairing should be lipstick. If your lipstick rubs off during a meal, there's little chance any relationship with fellow diners will be damaged by waiting until the meal ends to repair it in the rest room. If you are convinced you cannot survive a short time with natural lips, the very most that is marginally acceptable is to quickly—and I do mean quickly—touch up your lipstick.

Use only lipstick and a single mirror (not a compact that will spill powder, blush, and other paint). A dining table is not the place for a makeup overhaul. In fact a better idea is to use foundation and powder your lips when using lipstick. Then, blot them well before you eat or drink. This preserves your appearance and your dignity quite well. It also helps prevent unsightly and unappealing lipstick marks on glasses and cups.

Napkins

Q. ***Why must I keep my napkin on my lap? When is it proper to tuck it in at the neck?***

A. Really well-mannered people don't tuck their napkins in at the neck, but some small children and messy eaters do. A civilized meal is supposed to go at a moderate pace. You shouldn't need a napkin as a drop cloth for a feeding frenzy. Sometimes a bib is a custom at restaurants that serve messy foods like lobster. Generally, though, we graduate from bibs when we leave our high chairs behind. By now, I'm sure, you can navigate your food directly to your mouth without missing. Practice.

The reason for keeping the napkin on your lap is to avoid making your dining partners look at the remains of your tomato soup or spaghetti sauce drips and spills. Dining means more than just enjoying the way the food tastes. What you see and hear are important—and they should be pleasant. That's why it is better to bring your napkin to your chin for each mouthful with your free hand when you eat something messy rather than advertise that your soup seems to have a life of its own.

Unfortunately, old habits are hard to give up. Like a security blanket, there still are a lot of people, old and young, who prefer the not-so-smart bib method.

Q. *What happens when you don't put your napkin on your lap?*

A. You might get crumbs, soup, ice cream, spaghetti—or anything else that slips on its way to your mouth—on your lap instead. Etiquette rules are based on common sense. The reasons for using a napkin are logical, although modern-day needs for napkins are not nearly as dramatic as they were long ago. The status of today's napkins is pretty lowly. Most napkins we use are of the flimsy, throwaway paper variety. The first napkins date back more than twenty-five hundred years to the Near East. In those days meals consisted of several courses, and silverware as we know it had not been invented. All meals were eaten entirely with the fingers. This made a napkin the size of a large towel essential, and the first napkins were just that large. Later, the Egyptians, Greeks, and Romans called the towellike napkins *serviettes* and used them to wipe food from their hands. Today, if you go to Canada or England, they still use the word *serviette* for napkins—and call diapers "nappies." No matter what you call them, the rules for using napkins are the same. When you are dining at a friend's home, put your napkin on your lap as soon as your hostess does. That signals the start of the meal. Keep your napkin on your lap until you finish, then fold it loosely and place it to the left of your plate. If you must leave the table during the meal, put your napkin on the chair seat and push the chair back under the table. Never put your napkin back on the table until you've finished the meal.

Nose Blowing

Q. ***How do you blow your nose at the table?***

A. If blowing your nose is destined to be a noisy affair, you should excuse yourself from the table. If you simply have to tame a quiet sniffle and you have a handkerchief, just turn your head away from the people around you and take care of it.

Nose Picking

Q. ***Why can't you pick your nose at the table?***

A. Nasal secretions, commonly known as *boogies* or *boogers*, generally are green and slimy and therefore not especially appetizing to look at when you're eating. Nose picking is never, *ever* acceptable in public. That's why it just isn't done, particularly at the table. And if you don't use a handkerchief, you never know where those boogies will end up—perhaps on your neighbor's plate or under the table to surprise some unsuspecting hand that happens to be in the wrong place at the wrong time? Not very cool. Not very sanitary. Not very healthy. Not a good way to make new friends.

Other Countries

Q. ***Are table manners the same everywhere?***

A. No, indeed. Table manners in the United States will serve you well in North America and Western Europe. If you're going to Middle Eastern or Asian countries, you'll need to do some homework, which can be lots of fun because international dining habits are fascinating. You would learn you could belch to your heart's delight in an Indo-Chinese home and your host would be greatly complimented. Remember that good manners always get you far. That means that when you treat everyone with respect and kindness and it shows in your attitude, mistakes with dining differences in other places can be forgiven easily. The essence of good manners does not change, but etiquette (those *dos* and *don'ts* people usually confuse with manners) changes even within other countries.

Although basic table etiquette is the same within this country, in North America and Western Europe the dining traditions can vary widely. For example, Americans call the midday meal *lunch*, and it is usually a light meal. Most Europeans eat the main meal of the day at midday, not in the evening. *Midday* means different things to different cultures. To an American, *midday* means noon; to a Mexican it means about 1:30 P.M. or later. Americans consider the dinner hour to be about 7:00 P.M., give or take an hour. In Europe, the Middle East, and Latin America, dinnertime means as late as 10:00 P.M.

Pass the salt and pepper shakers together so they don't get lost or separated at the table.

Posture

Q. ***Can I put my elbows on the table?***

A. All of us have been told not to put our elbows on the table at one time or another. Some people—of all ages—believe that the only thing having good table manners means is keeping your elbows off the table. But that isn't half the story. In fact it is misinformation.

The reason to keep your elbows off the table when you're eating is that it looks and feels awkward. You run the risk of landing your elbow in your neighbor's soup if you slip. The rule is that elbows remain off the table while you are consuming food. However, when you stop to talk, it is very comfortable to rest your elbows on the table as you lean forward to converse. That's the time it is OK to have your elbows on the table—the only time.

Special Foods

Q. ***My family is vegetarian. What should I do when I am having dinner at my friends' houses? They are not vegetarians.***

A. Don't announce that you don't eat dead animals and make a face when your hostess offers you a hamburger. You can kindly refuse the meat if you wish.

If you are served meat without being asked, just don't eat it, but eat the rest of the meal cheerfully. If your host presses you to explain, say that your family doesn't eat meat and leave it at that. As long as you don't create a fuss, your host should respect your choice. Above all, be sure not to put your host through any additional trouble to prepare something special for you. That would be rude. It would be better to decline the invitation and ask to join everyone for dessert after the meal.

On the other hand, a good host always considers the preferences of guests. If you have guests at your home, be sure to find out if there is anything special about their habits. For example, do they keep kosher? Then be sure to tell whomever cooks your family's meals so that he or she won't be embarrassed at dinner.

Q. ***How do you get out of eating something you don't like?***

A. You could faint when it is served, but that would ruin everybody else's meal, which would be rude. Besides, nobody likes cold food. Seriously, though, when somebody prepares food for you—whether your mother or a friend—the time and effort that go into that preparation are true gifts. You don't have to scarf up every last morsel, but you do have to try to eat a little. After that you can sort of push it around on your plate and make it look as if you had more than you actually did. Think of how you would feel if you did your best to cook something and then nobody liked it.

Q. ***What do you do if you're given a food you've never had before, and you take a big bite and it is too gross to swallow?***

A. Oops! It looked delicious, but one bite and you can feel your eyes bulging out. Try to stay in control, calm yourself, and try—really try—to swallow. Chances are good it won't be fatal. If you absolutely can't, then quietly and without making a fuss, bring your napkin to your mouth and expel the food there, hiding it from others at the table. Then just go on with the meal as if nothing happened. Do not rush from the table with your hand clutching your throat. Do not say anything about the effect the food had on you. And, from now on, be more cautious about first bites. Try sampling a tiny bit of new foods.

Q. ***When you're ten years old, what's the right way to eat spaghetti?***

A. Spaghetti is my choice for the most user-unfriendly food. It is also delicious. Those long, thin noodles covered in rich, zesty tomato sauce are so good you naturally want to eat with gusto by gulping large mouthfuls at a fast pace. Unfortunately, this is not the smartest way to eat spaghetti. I once shared a spaghetti dinner with a group of adults. One was a "rapid consumer." The only time I saw his face was when he came up for air. When he did, it wasn't a pretty sight. There were little pieces of pasta and sauce splattered all over his hands, face, and shirt. He looked like one of Freddy Kruger's victims.

The people who know best how to handle spaghetti are its inventors. Italians swirl a small amount of pasta around their forks into a bite-sized portion with no loose ends to drip sauce. Less polished Americans have added to this method by holding a large spoon in the other hand and pushing the fork and spaghetti into it to mold the twirl (which, by the way, makes Italians wince). The trick is to start with a small amount of spaghetti, perhaps only three or four strands. You would be surprised at how large they become when they're twisted correctly. It takes practice, but when you get the hang of it, spaghetti becomes more fun and easier to eat.

Spills

Q. ***What do you do when you spill something on your friend?***

A. Princess Diana has done it. President Clinton has done it. Everybody has done it at least once, so relax. It is not fatal. The good news is that it was your friend instead of a total stranger. Whether you spill something on a stranger or friend, the same rules apply for making amends. First, apologize. Don't avoid looking your friend in the eye. Tell him or her how sorry you are. Giggling or making a joke out of it won't help; you'll only look foolish and irresponsible. Once you've apologized, take action. Clean up the spill as best you can without turning your friend's garment into a giant blotter. Provide your friend with an appropriate towel or napkin rather than making a fuss as you scrub her silly. If the spill is really bad, she should excuse herself and take care of it in the rest room. Offer to have the garment dry-cleaned and pay for it yourself—and then, by all means, do so. On the off chance that you spill something hot on a person, be sure to let your mom know so that she can check the next day to be sure there were no burns that required medical attention. If your spill did cause a burn, it would be your responsibility to handle the medical expenses, so be sure to alert your parents. But, for the most part, spills between friends, like laughter, are shared often.

Telephone Calls

Q. ***Should you tell people to call you back if they call during dinner?***

A. It is rude to abandon people at the table in the middle of a meal. Tell the caller you'll call back when the meal is over. Don't insist he or she call you twice. Then make sure you do what you said, and make the call. Keeping agreements is important.

Tipping

Q. ***Do I have to leave a tip, even if the service was bad?***

A. The short answer is yes. The amount of a tip should indicate the degree of service. Your starting point is 15 percent of your bill before tax for good service. Some people leave 20 percent or more for excellent service. Often these people waited tables when they were younger and remember how disappointing and discouraging it was to go home at the end of the day with virtually no money.

On the other hand, for poor service you can leave 10 percent or less. It is important to leave some percentage for the tip unless the dining experience was truly miserable, in which case you should tell the restaurant manager, who more than likely will adjust the bill in your favor. That would be an extreme case, however. Don't start going around complaining to restaurant managers to try to get free food.

For the most part, service people are paid below the minimum wage and depend on tips for the bulk of their income. If you and your friends almost die of starvation because you haven't gotten your cheeseburger and you haven't seen a server in so long that you forget what the server looks like, a small tip is appropriate. The reason is that even though the delay might have been caused by a mishap in the kitchen over which the server had no control, your server should have come by to explain the delay and to apologize.

By the way, when tipping began in this country, the money was placed on the diner's plate for the server before—not after—the meal. The word *tips* actually stands for "to insure prompt service." The United States is one of the very few places where the amount of the tip is optional. In other countries a percentage is automatically added to a diner's bill.

Incidentally, servers are not the only persons who should be tipped in good restaurants. Don't forget to give a dollar to the coat-check person for each coat and a dollar to the valet for getting you a cab or your car. Learn tipping practices early. Knowing how to be at ease in this situation will set you apart from most people.

If you can't afford the tip, don't go out to eat.

Q. ***My boyfriend always leaves a very small tip when we eat out. It embarrasses me. Should I say something to him?***

A. Servers work hard for their tips and often rely on tips far more than on their salaries. If the shoe was on the other foot, your boyfriend probably would tip more. However, give the guy the benefit of a doubt before you call him a cheapskate. Proper tipping is often a mystery, even for adults. The next time you're in a restaurant and the bill arrives, say something like "Our server really took good care of us. They work hard and count on tips more than salaries, so let's be sure to leave at least a 15 percent tip." Your friend probably will agree. Also remember that you should tip when you're at lunch counters. Even if you order only soda or coffee, still tip no less than 15 percent. If you order a meal at a counter, 10 percent is fine, but never leave less than fifty cents. Being a teenager does not relieve you of the responsibility to tip properly.

Here are some other tipping situations that are often overlooked:

For pizza or other takeout delivery service, tip two dollars if your order was moderately difficult and within ten minutes' travel time.

Washroom attendants should receive at least fifty cents if the attendant hands you a towel or performs a service for you.

Coat-check attendants should be tipped a dollar for each coat if there is no charge for the service. If there is a charge, tip fifty cents a coat.

Learning the rules of tipping will make generous, sensible tipping natural. It is a valuable skill that will serve you well as you get older.

Toothpicks

Q. ***Sometimes when I go to restaurants, I see toothpicks by the cash register, but when I use them my dad says it is bad manners. Why do they put them there?***

A. Toothpicks are truly wonderful. They can alleviate stress, soothe a short temper, improve one's appearance, and make your mouth more comfortable. What's bad about them is the way people misuse them. Mostly this falls into the category of wrong place, wrong time—for example, when you're having your class picture taken, when you're at the dinner table, or when you're talking and smiling, in short, whenever you're in public. Use toothpicks only when you're alone.

Utensils

Q. ***Why are utensils so complicated at fancy restaurants?***

A. Actually, they're not, but it's important to understand what each piece of silverware is designed to do. Utensils laid out in front of you when you sit down to dine provide very useful information. If you were in a private home and you saw several knives and forks, they would tell you how many courses you will be having and thus how to pace yourself throughout the meal. It is embarrassing to stuff yourself with the appetizer only to learn you still have six more courses to go.

If you are in a restaurant, the utensils are there for the same reason—to be used course by course. However, in a restaurant you can choose how many courses you wish to order. The server should remove the unnecessary flatware when you have made your selections.

Knives and spoons will be to the right of the plate. Forks and napkin will be to the left. Use utensils from the outside in, toward the plate, as each course is served. (In some cases you may find your salad knife and fork closest to your plate. This is a signal that, at a strictly proper dinner, salad will be the last course served before dessert. This is rare, however, since salad usually is not served after dinner in the United States.) If you mistakenly use the wrong utensil, just go on eating and ask your server to replace it for the next course. You won't find a dessert fork or spoon on the table if the restaurant provides finger bowls. They'll be provided later, with the finger bowls.

Q. ***I went to a fancy restaurant, and they gave me a fork and a spoon with my dessert. I didn't know whether to eat my cake with the fork or the spoon. What is the right way?***

A. If the cake has ice cream with it or a sauce around it, use both the fork and spoon. In the continental style of dining, put the spoon in your right hand and eat with it. Use the fork in your left hand to help push the cake and sauce onto the spoon. If there is no sauce or ice cream with the cake (or pie), there is no reason to use both. Leave the spoon on the table and use the fork. It also is perfectly fine to use just the spoon to eat cake with sauce and ice cream. The fork is just there to help you if you need it.

Waiters and Waitresses

Q. ***Several times, when I've been out to dinner with my family and guests, the waiter or waitress starts picking up dishes when one person is finished eating but the rest of us are not. I feel clearing dishes should wait until everyone is finished. What is the proper way to do this?***

A. The simple answer is that the server should clear all the dishes for each course at one time, when everyone is finished with that course. To do otherwise can embarrass both fast and slow eaters, which is rude.

However, dining with others is a cooperative experience. Whether you're a host or a guest, it is important to be aware of your dining companions and keep pace with them. Don't get too far ahead or too far behind. It also is helpful to know and use correct table etiquette that will telegraph to your server whether you have finished the course or are simply resting. You do this by signaling with your utensils, known as the silent service code. These signals are called the "finished" and "resting" positions for silverware.

The "I am finished" position should be used at the end of each course when a knife and fork are used. Visualize the face of a clock. Place the knife and fork in the approximate position of 10:20, the tips of the knife and fork at ten and the handles at twenty. The tines of the fork can be up or down in the finished position but down is more correct. The blade of the knife should face the fork. When eating only with a fork, place it tines up on your plate when you are finished.

In the "I am resting" position, the knife and fork are crossed on the plate with the fork over the knife with the tines pointed down. The fork tines face two and the handle faces eight. The knife tip faces ten and the handle faces four. Each handle extends about an inch over the rim of your plate. Think of the "I am resting" position as an inverted V.

A well-trained server never will remove your plate with the knife and fork crossed because he or she will know you're not finished. Remember that every server performs a delicate balancing act of timing the food with the chef and somewhat guessing that the diners will finish their courses at a reasonable pace. Here's where the balancing act that each good server must perform comes into play. Invariably, one person at the table is a slow eater (or a very fast eater,) either by habit or because of involvement in a conversation. Thus, knowing dining etiquette and a little bit about how restaurants work can help the meal go more smoothly for everyone.

Not all professional servers are trained to understand the silent service code. Those who are trained to understand it are usually found in more upscale restaurants.

Whispering

Q. ***Why is it rude to whisper at the table?***

A. Whispering usually means you're talking about someone within earshot and saying things you don't want that person to hear because it would hurt his or her feelings. Even though you might be saying something nice—like how cute the boy at the end of the table is—people usually jump to the conclusion that whispers are saying mean things. No matter what you're saying, if you hurt somebody's feelings, you're being rude.

7
Rites and Passages

"Courtesy on one side lasts not long."
George Herbert

For parents . . .

America is a ritualized society. Weddings, funerals, graduations, christenings, birthday parties, worship, and on down the list, each has its own set of rules of conduct.

The problem for children is that each ritual occurs infrequently. Each is new. They're surrounded by older people. They've never seen this particular ritual before. They don't know what to anticipate. The ritual looks bigger than life. The steps in the ritual look complicated and threatening. As a consequence children become nervous, and they dislike and avoid these group activities. Parents, unfortunately, usually don't make things easier. They expect their kids to follow the group, to understand and enjoy the ceremony (or at least keep quiet and respect it) as an adult with some experience in these matters would.

Be truthful with yourself. The first time you took your

child to a wedding, for example, did you explain in advance what he or she should expect? What the rite symbolized? Why people need a ceremony to wed? How long it would take? Who the people in the wedding party were and why they participated?

Picture yourself as a guest at a Masai tribe coming-of-age rite in Africa. You're offered a mixture of cow's blood and milk to drink in honor of the young tribesmen. What are the consequences if you do? What are the consequences if you don't? Get the idea of how children feel at a strange religious service?

The ultimate rite of passage is, of course, death. It is here that the etiquette of condolence proves the most supportive for young people. That's why it's important for them to learn it. When the reasons behind the ceremonies are understood (by teenagers, particularly), those ceremonies tend to permit peer bonding. Etiquette provides a way for teenagers to lead, to feel some control, to show friends they know what they're doing at a time when everyone else's emotions are in turmoil. I have a friend who, as a child, did not attend the funeral of her best friend's father because she did not know what to say or do. Her story is not uncommon. The value and beauty of knowing etiquette is that, had she known, she could have been present to comfort her best friend.

One of my advisers on death, grief, and condolence is Betsy Salunek, a certified crisis counselor, mental health worker, hospital chaplain, minister, and teacher. As she worked with adolescents in times of crisis, she noted that adults have the misguided notion that teenagers have great support systems built into their lives through their peer network. Nothing could be further from the truth. By definition, teenagers feel awkward, unable to fit in, and isolated between the worlds of adults and children. Usually their physical development races ahead of emotional maturity. Therefore their feelings are confused. When faced with the death of someone close, they isolate even further.

Additionally, Salunek points out, children are capable of feeling loss from the moment they're capable of feeling love. Witness how threatened an infant becomes when its mother leaves the room. Never forget that even young children need to understand at least some of the rites and ceremonies surrounding death.

Unfortunately, we live in a society where death is shunned. America denies the grief process. As adults we're supposed to get over a death in three days, the time most companies allot for funeral leave. The grieving process takes far longer, no matter how hard we try to contain it. As adults we must recognize these lengthy reactions to death and loss and communicate them to our children.

We also must tell our children to be prepared for unexpected reactions to death. They should know that they may display grief in surprising ways with quirky comments, unusual behavior, and potential bouts of unexplained sadness during the months following a death. In this chapter you will read a letter from a youngster who burst out laughing at his friend's funeral. He viewed it as a breach of etiquette, but he was certainly not the first or the last to do it. Salunek relates the story of her five-year-old granddaughter, who, at her great grandfather's funeral, stuck dinosaur stickers to his suit in the coffin and then handed out stickers to everyone she saw at the funeral that day. It was, Salunek explained, the way a little girl might be expected to express participation in, and feel a small measure of control over, her great grandfather's death.

If a good example is the best teacher, my own parents were exemplary. As an adult I've always been grateful that my father made it a point to attend funerals and viewings of family members, of his friends, of my friends, of his patients, and even of his parents' friends and families. As a youngster I chided him for being a "crate chaser." I said dead people would never know of his expression of sympathy. He remained steadfast in this practice, always inviting me and my sisters to accompany him if we knew the deceased or the family but never forcing us.

The return on those visits came to me when I was still a fairly young woman. Three close family members died within a month. The last died the week before Christmas. I don't remember how we got through the holidays. My parents were divorced, and it fell to me to keep things running. I do remember vividly, however, reading the guest register from the funeral home over and over, taking comfort in the names of the people who signed it.

I also remember that the impact of those three deaths never really hit me until the following Easter, when, as the new matriarch of sorts, I set the holiday table for fewer than half the people who had been there the year before. It was at that point I understood the difference between grief and mourning: grief is internal and private; mourning is external and social. As I went through both processes, I became more and more grateful that my parents had never shielded me from death or the rituals surrounding it, as so many of my friends' parents had.

I am grateful that my parents permitted me to ask questions about death and loss. They answered honestly, even admitting to ignorance on some topics. As a youngster I once asked my mother why she was so upset over the death of one of her friends. "I don't know. I just feel sad. It hurts," she said. Neither parent shielded me from the reality or the pain. Neither pretended the grieving process would be short or controllable. Most important, neither pretended I was impervious to the feeling of loss just because I was too young to know.

They also let me talk about death. Following the funeral

of a grand uncle, I crawled into bed with my parents and babbled about how frightened I was to die and to think about them dying. They listened quietly and did not attempt to talk me out of my fears or stop my tears. Instead they emphasized all the things my uncle had done with his life, how full and giving it had been. They never said things like "God took him." A child who hears that comes to believe God is terrible and to be feared because He takes away people we love. He makes the world unsafe. He makes people disappear.

According to Betsy Salunek, children can handle death and loss only in small pieces, spread over time. They will mourn and grieve, but parents may not recognize it, because after mourning for a very short while, for example, they'll run out to play. Their expressions of grief surface at odd times and in odd ways. Salunek suggests parents be aware of, and watch for, these oddities so as to create a suitable arena in which their children can express that grief. For example, a child may act out grief by playing "funeral" with dolls or by asking impossible-to-answer questions over and over, seemingly for no reason. It takes a wise parent indeed, she advises, to permit children to talk about their grief and loss and to have the opportunity to participate in the ritual of funerals. It provides children a rare way to express their unique relationships with the deceased as well as give them some measure of control.

To learn exactly what worries America's children about participating in these rites and passages, read on.

Funerals

Q. ***My friend died a while ago. I felt really bad when I went to the funeral. But when I got there, I started to laugh, even though nothing was funny at all. I was really***

embarrassed, and I didn't know what to do. What should I have done?

A. Above all, don't be hard on yourself. The most important thing is that you had the courage to attend your friend's funeral. That's a very difficult thing to do. I'm sure your friend's family was reassured by your presence, even if your behavior surprised even you. You did the best you could. What mattered most was that you were there.

Often, when we feel uncomfortable and ill at ease, we lapse into what looks like inappropriate behavior. According to psychiatrist Dr. James B. Hoyme, medical director at the Institute of Pennsylvania Hospital, your behavior was not uncommon, even for adults. It happens when people are put into anxiety-ridden, stressful situations. It is not uncommon for people who cry at funerals to walk away and be alone until they can compose themselves enough to return. If this happens to you again at a funeral, remember it would be OK to leave temporarily.

I've heard people say things like "I'm not going to the funeral. What difference does it make? He's dead anyway."

The truth is that it makes a big difference to the deceased person's family and close friends and to you. Funerals and viewings are important parts of the mourning process. Mourning is the outward way we deal with grief and loss. These rituals help us acknowledge the life the deceased has lived and the fact that it was cut off by death. You lost a friend. That's a very sad and difficult thing to deal with. I suspect there will be an empty spot in your heart for some time. Don't be embarrassed by that. Don't be afraid to talk about it with your friends and family. If you were close to the other people in your friend's family, talk with them, too. The truth is that it would be a great gift to them.

If seeing them again would not be possible or practical, you might want to write a condolence letter. In either case, remember that it is better for everybody to recount your friend's life and to talk about the fun things you did together or the things you especially liked about his or her personality. Avoid repeating how sad the death made you. You don't have to be maudlin to be comforting. For example, you might tell your friend's family about some funny things that happened to you both or remind them of some things your friend said that made for special memories. As you do this, you will find that gradually (very gradually) the sad pangs of remembering your friend will be followed by a sense of sweetness and gratitude.

Q. ***One of our classmates died. Most of us went to the funeral, but nobody knew how to act when we got there. We just sat still and didn't say anything. Now we wish we had done or said something. How should we have acted?***

A. The single most significant thing anyone can do when someone we know dies is to attend the memorial service or viewing, whatever form or religion that takes. Don't worry about what to say or do in unfamiliar territory. Trust that you will be guided by the church, synagogue, or funeral home officials. With kindness to the family as your motive for being there, you simply cannot err.

My father taught me this lesson by example, by ignoring personal inconvenience to lend support to the families of friends and colleagues whose loved one had passed away. As another friend of mine once said, "Everybody always worries about what to say to someone who is grieving at the viewing or funeral. When my mother died, I didn't remember a single thing anybody said to me. I remember only that they were there." Got it?

When calling at a funeral chapel, sign your name to the register so that the family will have a record of who was there. Briefly offer sympathy to the family of the deceased. Keep it simple and sincere. If the death was sudden, express your shock. If it was someone you will miss, say so. If there was a quality about the deceased that you found striking, admirable, or comforting, mention it. Don't linger. The grieving survivors will remember that you were there and that you said kind words.

Also remember that it is not necessary to view an open coffin. If such things bother you, don't do it. Instead, many people choose to pause to say hello to other people present. With them they can discuss memories of the deceased or even talk about other matters. Sometimes this "social" atmosphere that a viewing or wake takes on is disturbing to others. Usually it doesn't seem to bother the family. The important thing is that survivors remember that those who came cared enough to be there.

Religious Ceremonies

Q. ***I'm going to my first communion soon, but I'm not Catholic. What should I do?***

A. This is a big day for the child taking first communion. Lots of preparation will have gone into it. Dress nicely but conservatively. Wear a dress or jacket and tie and dress shoes. It is appropriate to give the child a gift. Don't give something silly or comical; this is a solemn occasion. Flowers would be nice or some potpourri or perhaps a lovely handkerchief or scarf.

You don't have to worry about what to do in church. You probably will not be the only non-Catholic there, and those who conduct the ceremony are aware of that. There will be plenty of clues to guide you. Just stand or sit respectfully when others do. You don't have to sing or kneel or take communion yourself. If you have a Catholic friend who is going, ask ahead of time what to expect. Perhaps you can go together.

Q. ***When I go to church with my friend's family, do I have to kneel when they do? I'm not Catholic.***

A. No, you don't. You may sit quietly in your seat if you don't wish to kneel. If you would feel more comfortable kneeling because everybody else is, there's nothing wrong with that, either.

Q. ***Do I have to pray in church if I don't want to?***

A. Any church is a house of worship, and its customs must be respected. You don't have to pray, especially if you are visiting a friend's church of a different religion from your own. Don't cause disruption or call attention to yourself. Simply be quiet and honor the rights of others to worship as they choose.

You should participate somewhat, even in a church of another religion. For example, if others are standing, you should stand. If others are singing or reciting, you should do the same. If others are praying, be still and bow your head. There is no reason to kneel, cross yourself, or take communion at a Roman Catholic mass if you're not Catholic. Some Protestant churches invite guests to take part in communion. If you wish to participate, that is entirely up to you. You should put some money in the offering basket when it is passed around. It will be your way of saying thank you for the hospitality you've been shown.

Q. ***We never say grace at our house, but at my friend's house they do. I never know how to act. What should I do?***

A. It is important to honor your friend's religion even if you believe differently. Not everybody says grace before meals. When visiting, it is a good idea to wait and see whether it is the custom of the house to say grace before starting to eat. If those around the table pause before the meal, leave your napkin on the table and don't touch your food or drink until grace has been said, no matter how hungry or thirsty you are. When the blessing is said, lower your eyes respectfully and think about the meaning of the words you hear. You may say amen (or whatever is appropriate) when it is over if you are comfortable doing that. Then pick up your napkin, put it on your lap, and the meal will begin. By the way, when your friend visits your house, he also should honor your family's customs.

Weddings

Q. ***I went to a Jewish wedding for the first time. I'm not Jewish. When I walked in, a man handed me a yarmulke. I didn't know what to do.***

A. The adage "When in Rome, do as the Romans do" certainly applies here. The offer of a yarmulke was a sign that you were being welcomed to share your hosts' tradition and culture, which is an honor.

In the Jewish faith, men wear yarmulkes in the tradition of demonstrating reverence for God in their places of worship. Following the lead of the other males in the group, you should feel free to don the one you were given. That's why they handed it to you. Of course, you did not have to wear it if you objected, and that's perfectly OK, too. However, it certainly would have been appropriate to follow and honor the tradition as a guest in a house of worship.

If you're wrong and admit it,
then you're right.

Q. ***I went to my cousin's wedding reception. They had place cards at the tables. I changed mine because I didn't know the people I was supposed to sit with. My mom got really mad when I told her. What's wrong with what I did?***

A. What you did was not a hanging offense, and I understand your logic. However, your mom was correct to insist that you should have taken your assigned seat. The tradition of arranging seating at a table (or at many tables for a wedding reception) usually is done with much thought and care. I'm a little surprised that you did not know anyone at the table. A host usually tries to avoid that. In any case, table seating is arranged in a way that ensures that those sitting at a particular table will enjoy lively conversation and a good time. You really never gave yourself the chance to meet new people. It might be that you were seated there because the host knew other guests at the table shared interests similar to your own. Even more likely is the possibility that your host knew you would like others at the table very much. You may even have been assigned to that table as a kind of "family ambassador" to assist others in feeling welcome and at ease.

For all those reasons, and others we may never know, it is important never to alter a host's seating plan. Trust that the arrangements were deliberate, not random. Do your best to be a gracious guest. You also can look at the place cards as a source of comfort. It is always a relief to know that you have your very own seat and don't have to join a table of strangers and feel as if you are intruding.

Q. ***My sister will be in her friend's wedding soon. Her friend also invited me. Do I have to give a gift?***

A. Wedding gifts are always wonderful to receive. They don't have to be elaborate to be meaningful. Technically speaking, you don't have to give a gift unless you were formally invited to the wedding reception and attend. If the bride-to-be casually invited you verbally to the church so you could see your sister participate in the ceremony, there is no strict reason for you to give a gift. If, however, you were invited to the wedding and reception with a formal invitation, you certainly should give a gift, especially if you go. Under the circumstances, a modest gift would be appropriate and in good taste, perhaps a picture frame or some dinner candles. Be sure to write a note wishing her and her new husband a healthy and happy marriage. Tell her how much you appreciated being included in the wedding festivities. Wrap your gift as beautifully as you can. Deliver it before the wedding or shortly afterward. Don't take it with you. It is an honor to be invited to a wedding. It's worth going all out to show your own thoughtfulness by what you say and how you present the gift.

Gifts don't have to be expensive to be precious.

Q. ***I'm going to a Quaker wedding soon. I've never been to one, so I don't know what to do. How should I act?***

A. Quaker weddings are quite different from traditional weddings. You're very fortunate to have the opportunity to go because they are personal, warm, and intimate.

The most striking difference is that no minister or priest is present. The reason is that Quakers believe that the divine spirit is present in all of us, and that we all are ministers, in a sense.

After you've entered the meeting house for the ceremony, take your seat wherever you feel comfortable. When everyone is seated, an official from the meeting will stand up and explain what to expect during the service. He or she will then sit down again and there will be a period of silence for a few, or perhaps several, minutes. At some point, the couple will break the silence by standing up and exchanging their vows. Then they will sit down again and settle into silence. That's when the people assembled are invited to stand and give their blessings. If you like, you would be most welcome to say your blessing for the couple. When the blessings are finished, the official who opened the meeting will "break" it by standing and shaking the hand of someone nearby.

There will be a marriage certificate for everyone present to sign, including you. You don't have to be a Quaker to sign it, and it is a privilege to sign because signing bears witness to the marriage and confirms that you have been a part of what's happened.

You can expect a reception following the wedding to be simpler and less elaborate than what many people expect wedding receptions to be. A Quaker reception is usually as personal and homey as the wedding itself. The entire experience is moving and charming, and you'll probably remember it for a long, long time.

I am describing the old-fashioned Quaker wedding here. You should know, however, that there are Quakers in the United States who have pastors and that if you attend that kind of a wedding it will be more like a conventional Christian wedding.

8
Correspondence

"When we want to express joy, grief, or gratitude, letters serve better than telephone calls. You can't reread a telephone call to reexperience the kindness."

Letitia Baldrige

For parents . . .

Of all the chores of childhood, writing letters is perhaps the most drudgery. It smacks of homework. It is hard to think of anything to write. It takes time away from play. It seems to serve no purpose. It often is forced on the victim, seeming like a punishment for having a relative, receiving a gift, or being invited to a party. Oh, why is that thank-you letter to grandmother for the birthday tie necessary? Perhaps it would all make more sense to children if they knew how much they, in turn, will appreciate being thanked in writing when they are older . . . but only if they begin the chain now and pass it on to the following generation.

In an age of telephone, telex, and computer modem, letter writing remains a powerful, although somewhat slower, means of communication from a distance. Rarity makes it all the more precious. Admittedly, people who understand

and use this power by taking the time to pen notes of every kind—thank-yous, condolences, congratulations, and support—are becoming like dinosaurs. It is too easy to pick up the telephone and call or, worse, assume those you should be writing just understand that you're too busy to do so but you're thinking about them anyhow.

In the world of etiquette and relationships, just "thinking about it" doesn't cut the mustard. Actions do. Giving your children respect for the written word and an understanding of the ceremonies surrounding it are great gifts. You should make their letter-writing lessons comfortable for their own ability levels. There is no pressing need that a thank you note from a seven-year-old be spelled and punctuated perfectly. If you're lucky, your child may receive the reward and reinforcement of receiving a letter in return, which will make it easier for the exercise to become self-perpetuating. Enthusiasm and encouragement for writing should come first; critiques can come later.

But all arguments about how correspondence becomes a life-enriching experience aside, the cold fact is that as adults we are judged by the quality of our correspondence later in the work arena. I believe there are two types of people in this world. The first enters a roomful of people and communicates through word and deed the message, "Here I am!" The second enters the same room and communicates, "Ah, there you are!" The latter is far more likely to become personally and professionally successful. The concern for the comfort and ease of others is the essence of good manners. Curiously, this attitude is most evident in correspondence. As Eleanor Roosevelt said, "A letter is a meeting between two people that depends solely on words." The real reason behind correspondence is to make those you contact feel remembered, acknowledged, and appreciated.

Everybody likes to receive mail, but few like to write. There are simple and easy ways to get your child started. Thank-you notes usually are the first hurdle (don't let your child send printed cards; that's a cop-out). Letters that say "Hello, I miss you" or "congratulations" or "I'm sorry" also are among the important early lessons.

And while you're teaching, don't forget that all-important lesson about the responsibility of answering mail, too.

You don't have to like a person to show respect. All human beings deserve respect.

Apologies

Q. ***I hit a baseball through my neighbor's window. He was really upset and angry. He's really old, too, and when I tried to apologize, he just grumbled. What should I do?***

A. Oops. Poor guy can hardly be blamed for being upset, can he? Sometimes older folks find communicating with young people frustrating because their hearing isn't sharp or the person they're trying to communicate with doesn't speak clearly. Since the personal approach wasn't successful, try writing.

You must apologize and make amends. Send a letter and

apologize again for the trouble you caused. It might read something like this:

> *Dear Mr. Smith:*
>
> *Please accept my apology for breaking your window the other day. It was careless of me, and I feel bad about it. I know all the trouble it has caused you. If you would like, I will repair the window myself. If you have made other arrangements, please send me the bill so that I can pay for the damage.*
>
> *Sincerely,*
> *Bobby Jones*

Remember that there is more to a letter than just words. Be sure that you use clean stationery. Write in ink, not pencil. Make a scratch copy first if you feel clumsy about writing.

The date should be at the top, on the right side of the paper. Start the "Dear Mr. Smith" below the date and at the left, a little in from the edge of the paper. Indent the first word of each paragraph about one inch. The all-purpose closing for just about any kind of letter is, *Sincerely.* It is especially appropriate for a letter of apology to someone older than you, or in a formal letter such as a business letter.

You'll probably want to deliver your letter by hand, since he is a neighbor. Even so, write your name, street address, and city and state with zip code at the top left corner on the front of the envelope. Your neighbor's full name, such as Mr. John Smith, goes in the center of the front of the envelope with your city and state underneath. Don't abbreviate the state name.

Properly addressing anything you send is a way to show respect for the person who will receive it. Never omit honorifics—*Mr., Mrs., Ms.*, or *Miss*—from an envelope. The only other word which can be abbreviated on an address is *Dr.* for *Doctor.* Write everything else out in full.

Condolences

Q. ***My friend's father died. I went to the funeral, but now I want to send her a letter, too. How should I do it and what should I say?***

A. Regardless of whatever else you have done—attended the funeral, sent flowers, paid a visit to your friend's home, telephoned—the condolence letter is a must. You should be congratulated for thinking of it. Such letters are comforting and diverting for those who have suffered a loss. Some even become part of a family history to be passed down to future generations. Forget about buying sympathy cards or condolence cards. They are impersonal and the easy way out.

Write your letter in ink. Use a fountain pen if you have one. A ballpoint will do if you don't, but it isn't very refined. Try to use black ink. If you own personal note paper, use it. If not, ask your parents for some good stationery. If your handwriting is hard to read, go ahead and type the letter or have someone type it for you. Sign it in ink.

What you write depends on how you feel. Write from the heart. Don't try to be formal; it comes out wooden and impersonal. At the very least, acknowledge your friend's loss. Say how sad you are about it. If you and your friend's father shared time together, mention that and any special memories of it. Say how much he will be missed. Offer your friend your help. The condolence letter is the place to recall in more detail the special characteristics of the deceased, visits to your home, lessons learned from that person, good times shared, etc. Such reminiscences celebrate the life of the deceased rather than being morbid and depressing about the loss. The shared memories of that life and times become treasured by the family of the person who has died.

Love Letters

Q. *My girlfriend moved to another city. She writes me all the time, and her letters always talk about love and stuff. How can I tell her to lighten up without hurting her feelings?*

A. Sounds as if your girlfriend just wants and needs reassurance that you care for her. She probably feels a little unsure of herself in a new city with no friends. She probably misses you because of that. You don't need to tell her directly to "lighten up." Instead, tell her about what you've been doing. If there are things you used to do together, let her know that you think about them by writing something like "I couldn't help thinking how much you would have enjoyed being there." Keep the tone of your letters newsy.

Talking to her directly also will make her feel included in your thoughts without the need for you to declare your undying love in blood. For example, you could write something like "I wish you could have seen David's face when he found out he aced the test he thought he had flunked."

Most likely, when she becomes more a part of her new scene, her letters also will take on a more newsy tone. Meanwhile, just be yourself. Support her. Understand that leaving everything you know behind is really tough, so she might be overreacting. However, even under the best of circumstances, writing love letters is chancy. You never know who could end up reading them. They could become a major embarrassment for everybody should they fall into the wrong hands. Personally, I think love letters are best written in the sand.

Pen Pals

Q. *I have a pen pal in Australia who lives on a vineyard. He writes the greatest letters. They are so good, I read them*

to my parents and friends. But I live in Raleigh, North Carolina, and I think my letters are boring. How can I make my letters more interesting?

A. First of all, Raleigh probably sounds pretty interesting to your pen pal because it is so far away. Don't give yourself a bad rap that you don't deserve. America is probably as interesting to him as Australia is to you. Also, the very fact that you have a pen pal indicates you probably are an interesting and curious individual. You probably communicate that about yourself without being aware of it. The funny thing about letter writing is that we all love to receive them, but we all think they're a chore to write. The easiest way to get started is to write the way you talk. Think of a letter as a one-sided conversation. Write the things you would say or ask your pen pal if you were together in person.

I think the surest way to make a reader yawn from the start is to write "How are you? I am fine." There are many interesting ways to start a letter. You might want to begin with something like "Last night I saw a television program about vineyards, and you came to mind. Your letters make me feel like I have real inside information." The goal of letter writing is to draw the reader into your written conversation as quickly as you can. You can tell your friend something you did that was exciting, fun, or wonderful; for example, "Today I went to Sea World and petted a dolphin for the first time. It would have been great if you could have been there, too. Do they have a Sea World where you live?"

It is much more interesting to write specific questions. They make the reader feel part of your conversation. Think about how you would feel if someone wrote to you and asked, "Have you recovered from the flu yet? What did you do when you had to stay in? Did you see anything special on TV? Read anything great?"

By comparison, think about how you would respond to "How are you? I'm fine." Both are basically the same questions. The difference is in how you ask.

Go ahead and use exclamation points or underline sentences or phrases if you want. In a personal letter these devices convey your enthusiasm. Steer clear of apologies for not writing sooner. They only make your letter sound like you're writing to fulfill an obligation rather than writing for the fun of it. Make your letter enthusiastic and full of your own personality. That will make your pen pal feel your letter was worth waiting for.

RSVP

Q. ***I got an invitation to a party. At the bottom of the invitation it said, "regrets only." What does that mean, and what should I do about it?***

A. *Regrets only* written at the bottom of an invitation means (strictly speaking) that if you cannot attend, you are expected to tell the host in advance. If you plan to attend, you don't have to call to accept the invitation.

However, if you were a host planning a party, wouldn't you want your guests to let you know one way or the other? Wouldn't you like to know that they were pleased to be invited and looking forward to coming? I know I would, so go ahead and do it.

Call the host and tell him or her that you received the invitation, how excited you are about the party, and that you plan to attend. If you cannot attend, do the same thing. Explain that you won't be there. Respond immediately to any invitation and be sure to stick to your commitment. Nothing is worse than holding out until the last possible moment in case you receive a "better offer."

RSVP is used most often on invitations. It is a request for a reply. It means "Respond if you please" in French (not, "Roast skunk very possible," as in the comic strip "L'il Abner"). If the RSVP is followed by a telephone number, just call the host. Sometimes the letters are followed by the host's address. In that case, send the host a short note right away. Indicate whether you'll be able to attend.

These guidelines will serve you well for most informal invitations sent today, the kind with casual wording on colorful, printed, fill-in-the-blanks cards. Formal invitations are a different story. They require a bit more homework.

It is important to respond to party invitations as soon as you receive them.

Q. ***I had a birthday party last month that was really embarrassing. I sent everybody invitations that said RSVP. Not everybody from my class was invited, so I didn't talk much about it in school. When the party came, some people who said they were coming didn't show up, and some of those who did come brought a friend. My mom was really mad. She didn't know everybody, and we almost didn't have enough food to go around. My mom said I should have called everybody to find out if they were coming. What do you think?***

A. What you've described here makes me crazy, just as it did you and your mom. You're not alone. The troublesome part is that people don't get much better at this as they get older and, presumably, wiser. Ask any adult who has given a party.

Your mom is right. The most reliable, but not foolproof, way to get an accurate guest count is to contact each invitee shortly after the date on which they should have responded (a proper RSVP invitation will indicate a time to respond, such as, "Please RSVP by July 12"). You can say something like "I haven't heard whether you're coming to my birthday party, so I want to make sure you received my invitation." That way you help them save face for not responding. You also have a pretty good chance of getting an accurate answer.

It is essential to respond to invitations as soon as you receive them. Anything else is rude. No fair waiting until the last minute to see if you get a better offer for that date.

On the other hand, if you find out at the last minute you cannot go to the party, you absolutely, positively must call the minute you know. Nothing is more rude than a no-show . . . except showing up with an uninvited "guest" unannounced.

The only time it might be OK to take an uninvited friend to a party is when you have a houseguest staying with you. In that case, and only if you know the partygiver well, call and ask if you may bring your guest along to the party. Remember that an invitation is intended only for the person or persons to whom it is addressed, period.

Signatures

Q. ***Why is it wrong to sign applications in pencil?***

A. A signature on a piece of paper represents your word, your bond, and your commitment. In other words, when you sign your name to a piece of paper, you promise that you are willing to be held accountable for all the words on that paper. By signing something we are saying that any statement above the signature is our responsibility and ours alone. It doesn't matter if the paper is a test, a letter, or an application. In the adult world your signature binds you to honor your agreement. Some examples are marriage certificates, leases, mortgages, bank loans, contracts, and credit cards.

If you are not willing to sign your name in ink so that it cannot be erased or changed, it is a signal that you are not willing to stand by your word. You would be very wise to think carefully about where you sign your name. Throughout history, verification of signatures has been a crucial factor in legal cases and criminal trials. Never take signing your name lightly or without understanding what you're signing.

Thank-You Notes

Q. ***My thank-you letters are boring, but my mother says I have to write them anyway. How should I do it?***

A. I know what you mean. Thank-you notes can be boring if all we say is "Thank you for the present. It was so nice of you to think of me." They're boring to write and boring to read, because they don't carry any of the spirit of the gift or the person who received it. But relax; help is at hand. Here is my three-step formula for writing effective thank-you notes:

First, be sure to thank the person for the specific gift and mention the gift by name. For example: "Thank you for the great electric blue sweater."

Second, acknowledge the effort and energy the giver put into selecting, purchasing, or making the gift. For example,

---

A wise person once said that those who thank promptly thank twice.

"You must have spent a whole day baking all those cookies."

Third, let the giver know how you have used or will use the gift. Write something like "I can hardly wait to wear it to the next school dance" or "The cookies will be a big hit at my sleepover tomorrow night."

Being specific and letting the giver know that you appreciate such generosity is the best way to share the gift with the person who cared enough about you to give it.

Q. ***My stepmother made me a sweater for my birthday. It looks OK, but I can't wear it because I'm allergic to wool. How am I supposed to thank her? Should I tell her that I can't wear it? I don't want to make her and my father mad. They live in another city.***

A. I think it's great that your stepmother spent all the time and effort to make you a sweater. That's the true gift, not the sweater itself. That's what to emphasize in your thank-you, whether you call her or write to her.

Since most of us like to receive mail and often save letters and notes to read again later, why not write to her? You can say something like "Thank you very much for the green sweater. The color is great. It must have taken a long time to make. I really appreciate your thinking of me so far ahead of my birthday so that I'd have the sweater on time." That way you're being specific about the gift and letting her know it is important to you.

It sounds as if she is doing her best to please you and let you know you're special. Don't hurt her or your relationship with words like "Thank you for the green sweater. Every time I get near it, I break out in a rash." Since it is unlikely that she will expect to see you wearing it because she lives in another city, there is no need to mention that you can't wear it.

If, by some chance, she does ask you, tell the truth. Repeat how much you appreciated the time and effort she put into making the sweater and tell her that when you tried to wear it your allergy acted up.

Do you have a brother or sister to give it to? If there is someone who could benefit from the splendid gift, give it away. Be careful to tell the person you give it to that it was a gift and you would love to wear it but cannot. That way you're making it clear that it is in no way a discard and that you continue to honor your stepmother's gift.

Holiday gifts deserve thank-you notes, too.

Q. ***Do I have to send thank-you letters to everybody who gave me a Christmas gift?***

A. The rule is that if the person who gives you the gift is there when you open it, saying thank you face-to-face is sufficient. That means you must send a letter to Aunt Millie for the sweater she mailed you from Pittsburgh . . . and anybody else who wasn't around when you opened a present they sent you. However, there is no rule against writing a thank-you note to anyone who gives you a gift in person, especially if the gift is something you really like. After all, wouldn't it please you if someone took the time to write a letter to you just to say what a big hit your gift was?

9
Etiquette and the Disabled

"Courtesy is a determined effort to consider others. The great secret is not having bad manners or good manners, but having the same manner toward all."
J. Carson

For parents . . .

It is probably the most vexing problem in the realm of human relations: how to avoid unintentional cruelty to a person whose life already has been touched by misfortune through trauma or accident of birth.

An attitude adjustment is the best start. Strictly speaking, a disability is simply a condition a person must adjust to and live with. Nothing more, nothing less. Able-bodied people tend to exaggerate those conditions with a "There but for the grace of God go I" attitude that pervades our language and behavior. I contend this attitude often is more confining than stairs without ramps or narrow corridors. Passing on these confining attitudes to our children is a great disservice.

America can learn much about developing interpersonal relationships with people with disabilities from its children.

This concept hit home the day I overheard a friend's little girl ask her mother if she could have a wheelchair, just like one of her classmates.

Ask yourself whether that little girl believed her friend had a "disability" at all.

A good beginning is to strike the word *handicapped* from your family vocabulary. It refers to days when persons with disabilities were relegated to standing on street corners, "cap in hand," begging for subsistence. Now the Americans with Disabilities Act of 1991 should change attitudes drastically. That law guarantees access to the workplace for some forty-three million Americans, this nation's largest minority. It is time for our children to learn the rules of conduct, for they surely will be using them in the workplace when they get there.

"Formal" etiquette in this area is slim but fast developing. It could be that we've paid precious little attention to these needs, that awareness has been low, and that the number of people in the "disabled" classification is expanding and demanding attention. For example, clinically obese persons are now considered disabled, as are recovering alcoholics in twelve-step programs. It probably is the prime area that proves the foundation stones of etiquette are kindness and common sense.

But in this category we need to add a third foundation stone—communication. If we admit to ourselves that we don't really know how to interact and assist those with disabilities, we also need to feel comfortable about asking directly so that they can teach us. Concurrently, those with disabilities must be willing to answer questions, to talk, to tell us what they need and don't need. Children, I find, are much better equipped than adults to do this without judgment or self-consciousness.

How can parents encourage their children in this direction? We can help them visualize the world through the eyes of others. Rent a wheelchair and let them ride around inside the house for an hour. Smear their sunglasses with Vaseline and send them off to watch TV or play a video game. The perspective they'll gain is another essential ingredient in etiquette. (And afterward you may want to help them express their gratitude for their own good health.)

You also can teach the simple fact that persons with disabilities have lives. They have families, jobs, hobbies, likes and dislikes, as you and your children do. The point is that the disability should not become the focus of the interaction or the relationship. That's boring for everyone.

However, the subject of the disability is definitely not taboo. Talking about it can lead to better communication, especially when it comes to understanding how to make persons with disabilities more comfortable or more efficient.

In the area of assistance, asking comes first. Never start "helping" without first asking. The need for help depends on the level of autonomy the person has attained.

You may assume, however, that interactions with most persons with disabilities will take more time. Be considerate. Expect and allow for it. Go slowly until you catch the correct pace. Eventually it will become second nature.

Watch your language. A person is not a condition. Don't refer to the condition when you mean the human being. For example, John is "the person with epilepsy," not "the epileptic."

Physical disability often carries with it extra baggage in the form of hardware that exaggerates our reactions—a wheelchair, a hearing aid, a white cane, and so on. A child's questions about relating to a disabled person often may concern the equipment. Children intuitively understand the linkage between a disabled classmate and a wheelchair. Adults may not.

Thus, set an example by being aware of personal space. Anyone who relies on a wheelchair, crutches, a cane, or a walker to get around will view that device as an extension of his or her body. Grabbing the back of a wheelchair and pushing someone without first asking for permission is as rude as pulling your spouse downstairs by the legs.

Likewise, "tidying up" by putting any of those devices out of sight when a disabled person is not using them creates a feeling of helplessness and lack of control. Be sure to keep them in view and as close to the owner as possible.

Persons with visual impairments may be physically but are surely not mentally blind. Vision loss comes in a range of degrees. If you're offering walking assistance, extend your elbow, not your arm, and wait. You may not be needed. If you are, this position puts you slightly ahead of the person you're helping to assure better balance. Give any verbal directions from the perspective of the person you're helping, not your own. Be specific. Say, "Turn right ninety degrees," not, "This way a little bit." Offer to describe the surroundings and do so in detail. If you're in a group, identify yourself and those with you. If someone leaves the group in the middle of a conversation, let the vision-impaired person know to eliminate the embarrassment of talking to thin air.

Hearing loss also varies by degree. Speaking loudly, to the point of shouting, may not be the answer. Instead, don't speak from another room where you cannot be seen. Make sure you have the person's attention before you speak. Face the light; don't put a bright light at your back, which shines into a hearing-impaired person's eyes. Don't eat or smoke when you're talking. With each of these gestures, you make lipreading more difficult. Minimize background noise. Speak slowly and clearly. For daily interaction with hearing-impaired people, learn American Sign Language.

Those with speech impairments may justifiably be insulted when people pretend to hear them if they don't. Don't be patronizing. It helps to repeat what you thought you heard so they can make corrections if needed. It is a kindness to ask questions that require only short answers. And, above all, allow time, don't rush, and never correct pronunciation.

Those are the basics. For the really tough questions about etiquette and the disabled, read what kids ask.

Be kind. You get back what you give.

Down's Syndrome

Q. ***My friend's little brother has Down's syndrome, and I don't know how to act when I go to their house to visit. He looks funny and acts weird.***

A. The reason your friend's brother acts weird is that children with Down's syndrome are slower to mature than other children. Therefore, they seem to act like babies long after they appear older. It is important to remember that they have the same wants and needs—to talk, to play, to be friendly, to have friends—as anyone. Treat him as you would anyone else. Just remember that he will have to work harder than you to succeed in life. The more everyone treats him with respect, the more he will succeed. So follow your best instincts. Never tease. That would be incredibly cruel to him and to your friend.

Hand Injuries

Q. ***I was in an accident, and now I can't open the fingers on my right hand. It is really embarrassing when people want to shake my hand, because I can't do it. What should I do?***

A. Once you decide on how to accommodate the situation and get used to doing it, you will relax. Right now it is especially awkward because you haven't figured out what will work. I suggest trial and error here, and don't worry about the errors. I've known several people in your situation. Here are some solutions:

You can warmly hold out your left hand to shake, keeping your right hand behind your back. This will signal to others that your right hand isn't available. I doubt anyone will question it. If you do get a quizzical look now and then, just say "I'm a lefty" and be done with it. Your explanation is true when it comes to handshakes, and there is no need for explanations or apologies.

Another approach is to reach out and touch people on the shoulder instead of shaking hands. Again, keep your right hand behind your back to eliminate confusion.

With either of these gestures you are communicating warmth for and acceptance of the other person, the essence of good manners. The point is that, once you become comfortable with your own style, so will everyone else. Above all, voice your concerns to those close to you. Ask for their help in practice sessions. The sooner you start talking about your challenge, the faster you can create a solution for yourself and those who care about you.

Hearing Impairments

Q. ***I don't hear well. If a person I meet says his or her name over and over, but I still don't get it, what should I do?***

A. This can happen to anybody. When somebody you meet gives you his or her name and you don't hear it, just say "Could you repeat that? I didn't get it." If, on the second try, you don't hear, say "I'm sorry. I still didn't hear your name. Could you say it again, please?" Then repeat it for the person to be sure you have it right.

If your hearing is impaired, don't be afraid or embarrassed to say so. It will eliminate confusion on both sides. If the person doesn't speak clearly, try asking for him or her to spell it for you.

Smile more often than you frown.

Here are two good hints for anyone meeting new people: First, once you have learned someone's name correctly, use it a couple of times in your conversation so that you remember it later. Second, when you are introducing yourself, it is really important to speak clearly, slowly, and loudly enough to be heard. If you have a name that is uncommon or difficult to pronounce, anticipate the difficulty by saying something like "I know it's a tough one. You pronounce it. . . ."

Q. ***Last week I was in the mall. I went up to a group of kids who seemed to just be hanging out to ask how to get to a certain store. When I asked my question, I learned they***

were deaf and didn't understand me. I was so embarrassed that I just said, "Sorry," and walked away. Now I feel funny about how I acted. What was I supposed to do?

A. You had the same reaction many, if not most, hearing people do when they encounter hearing-impaired persons. You got confused, scared, and panicky, and you fled. This happens a lot. Hearing-impaired people look the same as anyone else. You don't have any warning that you have to change your communication behavior until it is too late and you're in the middle of things. If this happens to you again (and I sort of hope it does so you'll have a chance to handle it differently and feel better), there are a few things you should do to communicate effectively.

Do your best, but don't worry if you're not perfect. Nobody is.

First, remember that hearing-impaired people usually are as interested in talking as anyone else. You don't necessarily have to vocalize to do that. For example, you could have taken out a piece of paper and written your question instead of walking away. You also could have gestured or "mimed." No doubt you would feel a little silly and awkward, but I guarantee they would have appreciated your efforts and tried to meet you halfway. After all, when you just shrug your shoulders, say you're sorry, and walk away, you make a person feel pretty unimportant, don't you?

Remember, too, that hearing-impaired people usually are very good at reading lips. If you look directly into the person's face and speak slowly and clearly, you may communicate quite well. Give it a try. Just keep in mind that speaking louder and louder until you are shouting doesn't help and embarrasses everyone.

Also keep in mind that hearing-impaired people are very adept at reading facial expressions and body language. You can get many points across that way without words. For example, raising your eyebrows signals that you're asking a question. And you don't have to hear to recognize confusion or fear on a person's face. Next time, try these suggestions. Everyone will win.

The best gift you can give is your attention.

Shut-Ins

Q. ***Our teacher from last year is dying of a nervous disease and cannot leave her house anymore. She lives sort of far away, and it is hard for us to visit her. What can we do to let her know we're thinking about her? We really liked her a lot, and we feel really bad that she's not going to get better.***

A. First, congratulations to you and your classmates for recognizing how important it is to maintain contact with those who are ill or otherwise unable to leave home. I realize your teacher's situation probably makes you feel strange and helpless, but now is the time she most needs to remain part of your lives.

The most important thing you can do is communicate, communicate, communicate! I would bet she would love anything you send her—cards, letters, notes, photos, tapes, anything. I have a friend, once very active, who also cannot leave the house. She used to be very interested in everything from window shopping to movies to new restaurants. I do my best to keep in constant touch with her. The way I keep our letters and phone calls interesting is to act like her eyes and ears once did, making mental notes of new and interesting developments to tell her. This kind of contact, personalized to the interests of the particular person, means much more than a card purchased in a store.

Tapes, either audio or video, are great communications gifts, too. Some are commercially prepared, like books on tape. They're pretty expensive, though. I think you could make a tape yourselves that she would like even better. Why not make a tape from the class? Give every one of her students a chance at the microphone or in front of the camera. You should set a time limit and tell them to prepare an interesting script in advance. Suggest strongly that they should say something more interesting than "Hi, Mrs. Jones. How are you?" Instead, give her some current information, like a radio or TV news report.

Have you helped someone today?

You could tell her about how you're doing in one particular subject or what subject you like most or least. You might read short passages from the school newspaper if you have one. You could even gossip a little, as long as it is the harmless, good-spirited kind.

Above all, if you're upset about her illness, share your feelings. Don't be afraid to say "I miss you" or "I'm frightened for you" or "I like you" or "You used to make me angry when. . . ." By being honest, loving, and caring you can give both of you a great gift.

Stuttering

Q. ***There's a girl I like a lot, but I'm embarrassed to meet her because I stutter. What should I do?***

A. This is actually a two-part question. The answers to both are simple—but not easy. There are often-successful therapies available now for your speech challenge. It will take some research to find them and some work to learn, but I know you'll decide it will be worth the effort. Talk with your parents and ask for help. Talk with your teachers and ask for guidance. Follow the program faithfully, work hard, and don't become discouraged.

Meanwhile, however, do not cheat yourself of the joy of meeting new friends. If you can be amiable and outgoing, chances are that most people won't even be aware of your stutter. Polite people will ignore it and encourage you to keep going. For example, have you noticed the good impression strangers make when they take the initiative and, yes, the risk of introducing themselves to those who don't know them? Most of us are grateful for another's friendliness. When an introduction is offered kindly, we are willing to overlook differences and suspend judgment.

Instead of being shy and shrinking back, introduce yourself. Look the person in the eye, smile, and offer your hand. You also might want to be sure that your grooming is perfect. That doesn't mean a new wardrobe. It does mean clean face, hair, nails, and clothing. Take pride in yourself.

Doing things carefully saves more time than rushing does.

Once you've met, show your interest in the other person by asking questions. Be sure to listen and appreciate the answers. We are so often nervous about meeting new people that all we think about is how nervous we are. Try to stop thinking about yourself and focus on the other person. This is the best way to get a relationship started and overcome embarrassment.

Above all, don't be ashamed that you stutter. Do your best to overcome it. Give yourself a pat on the back each time you stretch a little more toward your goal. And by the way, did you know that you're in some very impressive company? Actor James Earl Jones and British statesman Winston Churchill both stuttered and went on to become two of the most gifted orators of their times.

It takes more energy to understand people than to judge them.

Vision Impairments

Q. ***There is a girl in my church who is blind and walks with a guide dog. My mom says I should be friends with her, but I feel funny about it. What should I do?***

A. Many people, young and old, feel awkward in the presence of people who are impaired in some way. Usually the reason is that we don't know the best way to be helpful without hurting feelings. Here are some things to keep in mind when you start getting to know your fellow church member:

First, the correct term for a person who cannot see is *vision impaired*, not *blind*. Calling a person *blind* or *crippled*, for example, can hurt. And, frankly, it is less than accurate.

When you enter a room with a vision-impaired person, identify yourself immediately. Say something like "I'm Patricia. I come to the same service that you do here, and I was wondering where you go to school and where you live." That way you give her something to talk about right away. You also demonstrate your interest and friendliness.

When vision-impaired people introduce themselves, they enjoy shaking hands because it gives them a better idea of who you are. If she doesn't extend a hand, you should feel perfectly comfortable asking, "Shall we shake hands?"

Be careful to avoid petting the guide dog until you have asked and received permission. A guide dog gives a vision-impaired person freedom to move around with independence and dignity. Don't treat the fact that your newfound friend has a guide dog like a tragedy.

When you are walking with her, offer your arm and walk slightly ahead instead of taking her arm and attempting to steer her. When you come to a step, elevator, or other impediment, stop for a moment and briefly tell her what's ahead. When you offer her a chair, place her hand on the back of the chair.

Don't be embarrassed if you say some things without thinking, like "See you later." People with vision disabilities use these expressions. Whenever you are with a disabled person, be sure to speak directly to that person and not through a companion. Let the person set the pace for walking and talking. It is important to consider the extra time it may take for a person with a disability to get things said or done.

Finally, be polite to your new friend as you would any other and be confident that disabled people—just like anyone—place a high value on long-term friendships with those who are willing to understand and accommodate their needs.

Wheelchairs

Q. *Is there any wheelchair etiquette? What about the people who are in wheelchairs?*

A. Glad you asked. There sure is. First, for people not in wheelchairs:

A wheelchair actually is an extension of a disabled person's body. It provides mobility, just as legs do. When a person in a wheelchair is put in a position where he or she cannot move the wheelchair, the feeling is often one of helplessness or panic. Worse, when a person in a wheelchair is moved against his or her will, the helpless feeling is magnified. So, the first rule of wheelchair etiquette is to ask the person in the wheelchair if he or she needs assistance—and then wait for the answer before doing anything.

If you have a conversation with a person in a wheelchair, get to eye level. That could mean pulling up a chair or getting down on one knee. Too often we talk over someone in a wheelchair as if that person wasn't there.

Never pat someone in a wheelchair on the head like some sort of pet. The intention may be friendly, but the action actually is insulting.

Sometimes people in wheelchairs are able to sit in regular chairs at restaurants or other public places. If that happens, it is important to keep the disabled person's wheelchair in a place where it can be seen by the owner at all times. This is a kindness that prevents creating an inadvertent sense of panic. (The same is true with crutches or walkers.)

There is strength in being gentle.

For people who use wheelchairs, the most important etiquette tips probably are these:

Try to remain patient with inexperienced people who don't know what to do or how to act.

Be very clear and precise when asking for assistance.

Most people will have good intentions but inappropriate actions. Those with no experience or skill in dealing with the disabled need help and encouragement to do it correctly. Gradually the situation is changing, however. The Americans with Disabilities Act of 1991 has made a tremendous difference in attitudes and personal comfort levels by making it possible for the disabled to conveniently enter the workplace.

If you want more information on this topic, contact the National Easter Seal Society and request its materials.

10
Dining Out . . . for Adults Only

"The world was my oyster, but I used the wrong fork."
Oscar Wilde

If a good example is the best teacher, the best way to teach your children how to dine well in any restaurant is to take them out and set a good example.

Did that sentence make you cower in a corner? Don't worry; you are not alone. By far the most common request I receive from adults is for guidance in how to successfully negotiate a business lunch or dinner at a fine restaurant. The good news is that formal dining in America is the same in most situations, lunch or dinner, business or pleasure, at a four-star restaurant or the Italian bistro in the shopping center. Learn it once and you have it all.

If you have read the chapter on table manners, you have seen that most children don't have enough on-the-town experience to ask questions about restaurant dining. Learning formal dining is a go-slow process. Start with lessons at home during family mealtime. Don't try to cram; two lessons or so a week will raise their etiquette quotient quickly. At home you can teach about the proper use of flatware, correct posture, good eating habits, and general table courtesy.

But to get the big picture—how a restaurant works, what it feels like to be served, why there are several glasses and forks at each place setting, for example—children need to see it all, up close and personal. You'll have to go out.

Prepare the kids by explaining that you're taking them to dinner to see how much they remember of their home lessons. Tell them that you'll take the lead, that they should watch you to set the example. Make it an adventure. Do not criticize or chastise them for small mistakes. Guide them gently through big ones. Language like "Try it this way" goes down much better than "Do this." Make it a quiet competition for the best manners, with a small prize at stake as a reward for good conduct if you wish.

Every leader needs a good map. That's why this chapter is written for adults only. Read it once and you'll feel more comfortable the next time you go to a formal restaurant, with your boss or your children. Study it and you should be able to swing smoothly through any dining experience, in any company, anywhere.

We'll begin by examining the anatomy of a restaurant. Understanding how restaurants operate and how restaurant employees relate to you and each other will greatly increase your chances of having an enjoyable meal. After that we'll swing quickly through the mysteries of seating arrangements, the guest-host relationship, dinner conversations, passing dishes, napkins, tipping, and so on. By the end you'll be more than knowledgeable.

And if you get to a fine restaurant with your children and forget everything because you're so focused on not making the big mistake, remember that kindness toward others and your own common sense should see you through the meal.

Anatomy of a Restaurant

The structure of restaurants varies greatly from a showy Las Vegas–type dining room, to a casual California-style eatery, to a five-star French haute cuisine establishment. Just as restaurant styles are different, so too is protocol based on each environment.

It is important to understand how a restaurant and its staff operate. When you go to a restaurant, staff members actually become your employees for the duration of the meal. Smooth dining is a team game. Knowing how your team members work, what function each performs, and how they relate to you and each other will greatly increase your chances of having an enjoyable experience.

Maître d'/Host/Hostess: The maître d', who sometimes also is the general manager, and in smaller establishments, is often the owner, generally is in charge of all floor service. In busier restaurants, the maître d' will have an assistant manager who helps carry out the many responsibilities of the job. This job includes staffing, coordinating reservations with available seating, timing the flow of patrons to coincide with the pace of the kitchen staff, and handling special requests (like presenting an engagement ring or birthday surprise). The maître d' decides where your party will sit, handles complaints, and sometimes even serves the wine. The maître d' is a harried person with myriad responsibilities. Good ones never let you see their stress. It takes hard work and a solid team of assistants to make this job look easy.

Captain/Headwaiter: These terms are interchangeable. Not all restaurants have one. Captains or headwaiters supervise a smaller group of servers. If one person takes your order and another serves it, the person who took the order is generally your captain or headwaiter.

Chef: The chef is in charge of the kitchen and its personnel, how food is prepared, presented, and delivered to the table. In larger, busier operations, a chef is a supervisor and not necessarily a cook.

Bartenders and Servers: These are the people who directly serve you. They are supervised by the maître d'. Servers include waiters and waitresses and coat-check workers. Servers may also be referred to as *waitrons*, which is more politically correct, although I find the word disagreeable because it sounds like robots. Personally, I use *server*, which, like waitron, is also a non-gender-specific term.

Bussers and Dishwashers: The busser usually is the first person you see at your table, pouring water and providing bread and butter. Bussers are responsible for clearing dishes after each course, resetting the tables, and keeping the dining room stocked with necessary equipment such as china, linen, glassware (or crystal), and silverware.

Dishwashers work behind the scenes, cleaning up. You probably won't encounter them. They also are referred to as stewards. Bussers sometimes are referred to as server attendants.

Sommelier: Some restaurants have a sommelier or wine steward. This person orders wine for the restaurant and assists patrons in wine selection. In most restaurants today you're more likely to find the maître d' performing this function.

Each of these employees works to produce one result: a gracious and satisfied customer who will return regularly. But each team member is motivated by different needs. The maître d' wants everything to run smoothly, efficiently, and profitably. Servers, bartenders, and bussers are motivated by anticipated tips and recognition for a job well done. Chefs are motivated by praise for their taste and creativity. Chefs have a well-earned reputation for being fussy. If you visit one restaurant regularly, it pays to praise the chef if warranted. It's a good idea to ask to meet the chef to give personal congratulations or to send your message of appreciation through your server.

Table Manners

Table manners are the same whether you're attending a business or social function. For children, however, you may need to explain that it is more important to pay attention to conduct when dining out. After all, it is in a public setting, and the sensitivities of other diners must be considered. More important (although you'll have a difficult time convincing your offspring of this), good table manners prepare children for a successful adulthood. There is an unspoken but very real prejudice against people with bad table manners. In a 1993 poll for *USA Today*, poor table manners ranked fourth on the list of America's "worst dating turnoffs" after vulgar language, no sense of humor, and poor conversational skills. The *Wall Street Journal* in 1993 published an article that estimated that 30 percent of all job interview failures could be attributed to poor manners.

General Demeanor

• Sit down and stand up from the left side of the chair unless there is a major obstruction. Men traditionally pull out chairs from the right side to help seat a woman. This makes it practical and easy for the woman to sit down and rise from the left side without bumping into others.

• Put handbags, briefcases, keys, eyeglasses, gloves, and anything that isn't part of the meal on the floor, not on the table. Stow these hazards out of the way of foot traffic. Safety and common sense are basic tenets of etiquette.

• Sit back a few inches from the table. Sit up; don't slouch. Don't lean back or tilt your chair.

• Keep elbows off the table while you're eating, with hands

generally in view. It's fine to rest your elbows on the table when conversing between courses or after the meal is finished.

• If you need to comb your hair, straighten your tie, apply lipstick, or dislodge food with a toothpick, excuse yourself and leave quietly for the washroom. Don't do it at the table.

• When someone leaves the table, don't ask where they're going and don't volunteer directions to the washroom.

• Don't smoke before or during a meal. If you're sitting in a smoking section and it's acceptable to all others at your table, light up after dessert.

• Taking medicine or vitamins is best done discreetly, away from the table. If you must take medicine at the table, don't complain about the size of the tablets or the difficulty swallowing them. Don't explain why you need to take medicine; don't ask if someone else does. A restaurant is no place to lay out an array of vitamin supplements to show how well you take care of yourself, either.

• If you spill or break something, don't make a big issue of it. Quietly get the waiter's attention. Blot whatever you can. Permit any victims of the mishap to take care of themselves. Do not dip your napkins into the water glass to wipe off a food stain. If your accident seriously stains someone's clothing, offer to pay for dry cleaning.

• Try not to belch, but if it happens, cover your mouth with your napkin and quietly say "Excuse me" to no one in particular.

• Be natural. Avoid affectations or attempts to mimic what you've seen portrayed in films as "sophistication." Don't pretend to understand menu items written in French if you don't (ask your server; that's what they're for). Don't try to order with a perfect Italian accent if you don't speak the language. Don't be a wine snob. These affectations are a parody of good manners, not the real thing.

• It isn't necessary to thank the server or busser repeatedly for doing a good job. If you are being served while talking, don't stop. Let the service be unobtrusive and let your tip reflect your thanks.

• Keep up your end of the conversation.

• Pace your eating to that of others at the table. Try to finish each course as others do.

• Ordering alcohol, including wine, is a matter of personal preference. If you do, control your intake. There is no need to apologize if you don't drink alcoholic beverages. Never encourage a dinner guest to drink; you don't know his or her personal history. If you prefer nonalcoholic beverages, order without explanation, justification, or apology. If you are the host, don't let your guests drink alone; order something, alcoholic or not. If a guest asks if you're having a drink and you are not, say something like "I'm not having wine today, but please do if you would like." The word *today* erases any perceived judgment by either party about alcohol consumption. It says you might have had some yesterday and perhaps plan to tomorrow.

Ordering

• If your menus have not been delivered when you are seated, ask for them when you order the first round of drinks.

• Take a time-out to focus on ordering the meal. If you're a regular at this restaurant, mention personal favorites. Don't be shy about making suggestions for appetizers and main courses. This indicates your desire to help your family order whatever they would like. Permit your server to take everyone else's order first. Try to help everyone order the same number of courses so that you all dine together. No one is comfortable eating alone.

• If your children are unsure about ordering on their own, encourage them to ask you "What's really good here?" or "What do you recommend?"

Ordering Wine

You may want to introduce your children to the ritual of ordering wine to be filed away for use later in adulthood. Here is the routine:

• Red or white? When the sommelier or server comes to take your wine order, ask your group which they prefer. If most are drinking red to accompany a main meat course, but one guest is having fish and might prefer white, offer that person white wine by the glass (and a second when that is finished) while ordering a red by the bottle. If the group is split evenly, order a bottle of each and, if there is demand, reorder whichever is consumed faster.

• A bottle of wine is uncorked at the table by the sommelier or server. A small amount (about two ounces) will be poured for the person who ordered it, who then checks the wine for clarity, color, bouquet, and taste. If the wine is satisfactory, the sommelier will then pour glasses for the guests, ladies first, ending with the person who made the selection. Often the cork will be presented. Examining the condition of the cork sometimes can indicate the integrity of the wine. If the cork is overly dry and crumbling, or if it is soaked with wine when squeezed, it may mean that too much air has gotten into the bottle and turned the wine. You also may see people sniffing the cork to ascertain the bouquet of the wine. Cork smells like cork, so it makes more sense to smell the wine itself.

Conversation

• Dining out with the family is a social occasion. Good conversation makes it so. Steer your children away from argumentative topics. Lead them to current events, school, sports, hobbies, or cultural topics. Listen to what they say and show interest.

• No mean-spirited gossip. Adult topics like politics or

finance can be very educational for children as long as the conversation remains within their grasp and they're given the chance to respond and react, just as in a conversation between adults.

• Support continuing conversation with open-ended questions such as "How do you feel about . . . ?" or "What is your opinion of . . . ?" Avoid questions with yes-or-no answers; they can stop a conversation cold.

• If you remember that the main purpose of dining together as a family is to improve your relationships, you can't go far wrong in conversation.

• Be a good listener. Don't interrupt.

Napkins

• In fine restaurants, servers usually unfold and place napkins on each lap. If not, you should take the lead, usually immediately after being seated, by doing it yourself.

• The most important thing to remember about a napkin is to use it by dabbing your mouth, not wiping. Don't wave it like a flag. Don't use it to clean utensils or your eyeglasses. Don't blot your lipstick with it. Don't use it as a handkerchief.

• Your napkin belongs on your lap, not around your neck or on your chest.

• Large dinner napkins remain folded in half on your lap, with the fold closest to your body. Small luncheon napkins should be opened completely.

• If you leave the table during the meal, put your napkin on the chair and slide the chair under the table. Do not toss it on the table.

• When the meal is over and you're ready to leave, pull the napkin from the center through an opening between your thumb and forefinger and leave it to the left of your plate. Don't try to refold it.

Flatware

• If your flatware is dirty, ask your server for replacements.

• If you drop a utensil, leave it. Ask for another.

• Don't wave cutlery in the air to punctuate your conversation.

• Flatware can be used to signal your server about whether you're finished with the course or just resting. This is called the *silent service code.* In the rest position, the knife and fork are crossed on the plate with the tines pointed down. The fork tines face two and the handle faces eight on the clock. The tip of the knife faces ten and its handle faces four. Each handle should extend about an inch over the rim of the plate. A well-trained, savvy server will not remove your plate with the fork and knife crossed because he or she will know you're not finished. Think of the rest position as an inverted V. Remember that the knife blade always faces in.

If you're finished with the course, place knife and fork in the 10:20 position. The tip of the knife faces ten while its handle faces four on the clock. The fork is placed tines down, next to the knife in the finished position. The knife blade faces in toward the fork. Using this position makes it easier for a server to clear your plate from the right. The server can anchor your fork and knife handles with his or her thumb so that they don't slip.

• The number of utensils at a place setting depends on the number of courses to be served. There will be one or more utensils per course. At some very formal restaurants, servers may replace flatware prior to each course.

• Knives and spoons will be to the right of the plate. Forks and napkin will be to the left. Use utensils from the outside in, toward the plate, as each course is served. (In some cases you may find your salad knife and fork closest to your plate. This is a signal that, at a strictly proper dinner, salad will be the last course served before dessert. This is rare, however, since salad usually is not served after dinner in the United States.)

- If you mistakenly use the wrong utensil, simply go on eating and ask your server to replace it for the next course.

For more information on table manners, refer to *Letitia Baldrige's New Complete Guide to Executive Manners* (Rawson Associates, 1993) or *Letitia Baldrige's Complete Guide to the New Manners for the '90s* (Rawson Associates, 1990).

Eating Habits

- Dining out with the children is a great time to experiment with new dishes that they may never get at home or have the courage to order for themselves.
- The host should begin eating first. That will be the signal for everyone else to start.
- Lift food to your mouth. Don't bend over the plate and shovel it in.
- Keep your mouth closed when you chew. Don't talk with food in your mouth.
- Take easily manageable bites. Swallow before taking a sip of beverage.
- Scoop soup away from you so that any drips will fall into the bowl, not on your lap. Use the soupspoon. Sip from the side of the spoon. Don't drink from the bowl (an exception may be clear consommé served in a bowl with handles intended to be picked up and sipped). Crackers should be eaten on the side, not crumbled into the soup. Don't blow on soup (or any other food or drink) to cool it. Wait a bit and then dip from the side of the bowl, where it cools faster naturally.
- A pat or slice of butter goes on your bread plate or the edge of your dinner plate rather than directly on the bread or roll.
- Break bread with your hands. Don't cut it with a knife.

Butter a bite-size piece at a time. Never butter a whole slice of bread or an entire roll all at once.

• Don't eat with your fingers at a restaurant unless common sense dictates otherwise. (This rule is lifted at a cocktail party or barbecue.) At the table, even fried chicken is eaten with a knife and fork. It is fine to remove fish bones from your mouth with your thumb and index finger and then put them on the edge of the plate.

• Don't dunk.

• Don't crunch ice in your mouth.

• If you find something objectionable in your mouth like gristle, use your fork to remove it discreetly. Deposit it on the plate and camouflage it under ornamental lettuce. Pits and seeds can be removed from your mouth with your fingers.

• Glasses containing red wine are held around the bowl; the warmth of your hand helps release the bouquet. Glasses of white wine or champagne are held by the stem to help keep them cool.

• If sugar or sweetener is served in packets, tuck the empty paper under the edge of a saucer or place it in the ashtray if no one will be smoking.

Passing Food

• Pass to your right.

• Pass each item that goes with each course at the start of the course (even if you're not having any).

• Pass the cream and sugar by placing them on the table to your right within reach of the next person. Gravy boats, pitchers, and creamers should be placed with the handle facing the next person.

• Don't reach. If you want something out of reach anytime during the meal, ask someone to pass it to you.

• Be attentive for passing requests. Dining is not an "every man for himself" experience.

Closing the Meal

• After the salad and main course, the table will be cleared and the maître d' or your server will return with a dessert menu or cart. Encourage dessert, but don't push. If others order dessert, get something for yourself, even if it is fruit.

• Coffee usually is offered with dessert. Children may want juice or another glass of milk.

• Ask for the check when the coffee is served.

• Don't pat your tummy, loosen your belt, or otherwise report to the table your degree of fullness after a meal.

Paying the Bill

• Settle quietly at the table. Don't scrutinize the bill. Don't pull out a pocket calculator. If you notice a discrepancy, handle it away from the table with the server or maître d'.

• If you are paying with a credit card, don't forget to add tips for the staff. If you are using cash, don't toss it on the table. Use the tray or folder in which the bill is presented.

• Mothers should pay the bill once in a while to set an example for daughters who surely will have to handle this job from time to time as adults.

Tipping

• Even if you use a credit card, carry some cash for tips.

• If you are a regular at a restaurant or if you have gotten exceptional service, it pays to take care of the maître d' if you plan to return. A maître d' who provides you with a great table for a special event or oversees a smooth-running business meal should receive ten to twenty dollars, depending on the size of your group and the complexity of your special requests.

• A captain or headwaiter (the person who takes your order and may or may not serve you a course) should get 5 percent of the bill either in cash or specified on the bill if you use a credit card.

• Your server should get 15 percent or more of the bill, according to the level of service provided. Remember that your tip to the server usually is divided among the entire service team. Bartenders and bussers probably will share in some percentage of your tip.

• Your sommelier (wine steward) should be tipped 15 percent of the wine bill if he or she performs special services (like helping you choose the right wine for your meal) other than opening the bottle.

• Coat-check workers should receive one dollar for each coat.

American and Continental Dining Styles

These terms refer to methods of holding and using utensils.

In the American style the knife is used for cutting only. It is held in the right hand (for right-handers). The left hand holds the fork for stability. The knife is then put down on the edge of the plate (blade edge facing in), and the fork is switched to the right hand to lift the cut piece to the mouth. Americans are the only people in the world who use this zigzag style of dining. Hands rest in one's lap when they are not being used.

In the continental style the knife remains in the right hand and the fork in the left. After the food is cut, the knife is used to push it onto the fork. The tines of the fork face downward when the cut food is lifted to the mouth unless the type of food requires otherwise (for lifting peas or creamed foods, for example). Hands remain above the table from the wrist up when they're resting and not in use.

Either style is acceptable as long as you don't switch back and forth during the meal. Personally, I find continental style more simple and graceful.

When you take your children out to dinner, act as their host. Your ability to be comfortable and relaxed will reflect directly on them and their enjoyment of the lesson. Have confidence. Know what you're doing. Only then will you be able to make your young guests feel welcome and at ease.

Index